A STRAIGHTFORWARD GUIDE
TO
JOB AND CAREER OPPORTUNITIES
2nd Edition
Jeanette Benisti

D1322104

Contents

Introduction

Introduction

Choosing the right career constitutes one of the most important decsions that a person can make, whether you are young, i.e. a school leaver or a graduate or whether you are older and looking for a career change.

This book deals with the main areas of employment and offers a breakdown of a number of key jobs within that field plus also the main contacts for you if you choose to further your line of enquiry. A main contact number and website is also included so that you can discuss the wide range of careers on offer that are not listed in this book. To list every career on offer, and do the main jobs justice, which has been done in the various sections, is beyond the scope of this book.

We have listed 21 main areas of work in the book, that encompass most careers, including: accountancy; advertising; the armed forces; banking and finance; catering; civil service and local government; construction; engineering; farming and land jobs; health service; information technology; journalism and printing; the legal profession; marketing; music radio and tv; the police force; retail; social work; sport and liesure; teaching; travel and tourism and vetinary.

Out of these areas you are sure to find a career that might suit you and your particular skills and abilities, plus what you want to devote your working life to.

Some people look for money, regardless of the job and others look for a more socially orientated job, one that provides a degree of material reward but also provides greater personal satisfaction.

The National Careers Service website https://nationalcareersservice.direct. gov.uk provides very useful information on career choices and also outlines a wide variety of jobs.

Good luck with your career search.

Jeanette Benisti
October 2012

1. ACCOUNTANCY

This section covers:

* The Accounting profession
* The Actuarial Profession

Mention accountancy to people, particularly non-accountants, and they groan. Accountancy is perceived as a very conservative and rather boring profession. However, it is anything but. Accountancy is at the heart of all business and is a great way to learn the machinations of any industry whatever it may be. It is also a profession that pays well.

Accountancy is central to all business, whether large or small. The complexities, however, change with the nature and size of businesses and their environments.

An accountant is involved in the financial transactions of particular businesses and also the preparation of accounts and also auditing. Accountants deal with a wide variety of areas, such as taxation, business forecasting, business modelling, financial performance, investments and acquisitions and mergers. Because the work is so diverse accountancy is split into specialist areas, in the main three specialist areas.

MANAGEMENT ACCOUNTING

The nature of the work
Management accountants work mainly in commerce and industry. There work is integral to a company's operation, dealing with planning budgets, monitoring ongoing expenditure and preparing reports for external bodies. Management accountants may be qualified Chartered Accountants, Chartered Certified Accountants or Management Accountants.

ACCOUNTANTS IN PRIVATE PRACTICE

As the name suggests, accountants working for private practice will offer their services to all types of business, small organisations, fee paying clients and so on. Basically, they are freelance. They are either qualified as Associate Members of the Institute of Chartered Accountants in England and Wales (CAEW), the Institute of Chartered Accountants in Scotland (CAS), The Institute of Chartered Accountants in Ireland (CAI) or the Association of Chartered Certified Accountants (ACCA).

PUBLIC SECTOR ACCOUNTANTS

This is a different area of accountancy, employing the same essential skills but operating in a very different environment which encompasses local and national government finance. Public Sector accountants control and assess the expenditure within local authorities, health trusts, universities and central government. As you can imagine, this is a complex and varied area of accountancy.

Entry requirements

Most trainee accountants are graduates. maths is obviously an important element of accountancy and if you have a degree which involves maths, for example business studies, this will stand you in good stead. Most employers will set numeracy tests as part of the overall selection process. There are other entry requirements, for example, some professional bodies mentioned above, before accepting a person onto their trainee programme will require 5 GCSE's grades A or B and two A levels as a minimum.

Accountants who are qualified with any of the professional bodies can practice in the public sector. However, the most relevant organisation is the Chartered Institute of Public Finance and Accountancy (CIPFA). If, however, you don't have another accountancy qualification you must, as a minimum have three GCSE's Grade A to C and two A levels. Maths and English will be a requirement.

The best advice is to identify which area of accountancy most attracts you, identify the relevant professional body and then make enquiries about entry qualifications. The most important thing is to gain a job in the appropriate area and then, through the employer, gain day release onto the required course.

What can you earn?

Salaries within the accountancy profession will vary with industry and location, also size of the firm. As a trainee you can expect £24,00-£28,000 in London and the South east, with starting salaries varying elsewhere. After qualifying salaries will increase significantly. A good accountancy qualification will always hold you in good stead.

Other areas of accountancy

A less qualified area of accountancy is that of accountancy technician. Accountancy technicians work in a variety of roles, usually assisting qualified Chartered Accountants. There are no set entry level qualifications but people wanting to work within this area must be confident in maths. Good IT skills are also valuable as Information technology is integral to accountancy. Salaries are lower than qualified accountants but can still be attractive.

More information

The following are the important bodies within accounting and they can offer all the advice that you will need.

Chartered Institute of Management Accountants (CIMA)
0208 8849 2251
www.cimaglobal.com

Chartered Institute of Public Finance Accountants (CIPFA)
020 7543 5600
www.cipfa.org.uk

Association of Certified Accountants
020 7059 500
www.accaglobal.com

Association of Accounting technicians (AAT)
0845 863 0800
www.aat.org.uk

ACTUARY

The nature of the work

This is a distinct area of finance, dealing with the assessment of financial risks and probabilities. Typically, you might find actuaries working in areas such as pension forecasting, life assurance and other areas of insurance. They will also be involved in other areas of business where risks are involved. Actuaries will use their skills in mathematics and statistics to create models to analyse past events and predict future outcomes. Actuaries can be found either in private practice, typically consultancies and also government and the health service.

Entry requirements

To qualify as an actuary you must become a student member of one of the professional bodies, which are either the Faculty or the Institute of Actuaries. Minimum qualifications for entry are usually three GCSE's Grades A-C including English and two A levels one of which must be maths at grade B. If you have a second class honours degree in any subject then a grade C in maths is usually acceptable. If you have a degree in maths or actuarial science you do not need maths A level.

Once you have completed your professional training you become a fellow of either the Institute or Faculty. To become a Fellow you must pass 15 professional examinations. Depending on your prior qualifications you may be exempt from some of the exams at the Core technical stage and some at the other stage.

What can you earn?

Actuaries earn high salaries, with a trainee beginning at around £30,000. This will rise significantly as training and qualifications progress.

More information

The Association of Consulting Actuaries

020 73824954
www.aca.org.uk

Faculty of Actuaries
0131 240 1300
www.actuarites.org.uk

Financial Services Skills Council
020 7216 7366
www.fssc.org.uk

Government Actuaries Department (GAD)
020 7211 2601
www.gad.gov.uk

The Actuarial Education Company
01235 550005
www.acted.co.uk

2. ADVERTISING

Advertising is a very attractive profession. It is also a complicated profession and if you get it right it can provide enormous benefits both to an employee but also clients. It can be a very worthwhile career. In this section, we cover the following:

- Advertising account executive
- Copywriters

Their are numerous other positions within advertising, for more information contact:

Institute of Practitioners in Advertising (IPA)
44 Belgrave Square
London
SW1X 8QS
Tel: 020 7235 7020
www.ipa.co.uk

ADVERTISING ACCOUNT EXECUTIVE

The nature of the work
As an account executive, you would find out about the client's advertising goals then work with your agency's creative and planning staff to ensure that effective advertising campaigns are produced.

Your tasks would include:

- meeting clients to discuss their advertising needs
- working with account planners to come up with a campaign that meets the client's brief (instructions) and budget
- presenting campaign ideas and costs to clients
- briefing the creative team that produces the words and artwork

- negotiating with clients, solving problems and making sure that deadlines are met
- checking and reporting on the campaign's progress
- keeping in contact with the client at all stages of the campaign
- managing the account's budget and invoicing the client
- trying to win new business for the agency.

You would normally handle about three or four accounts at the same time.

What can you earn?

Starting salaries are around £18,000 to £24,000 a year. With experience, this normally rises to between £30,000 and £45,000 a year. Top salaries can reach £90,000 a year.

Entry requirements

Employers will usually be more interested in your personal qualities, such as creativity, quick thinking and business sense, than your formal qualifications. However, competition for jobs in advertising is very strong so it may help you if you have a BTEC HND or degree in one of the following subjects:

- advertising
- marketing
- statistics or operational research
- communication and media studies
- business or management
- psychology.

Any previous work experience that you have in communications, marketing, sales or the media would also be useful.

In smaller advertising agencies you may be able to start in a more junior position such as administrator, and work your way up as your experience in the industry grows. It is a good idea to try to find work experience in an advertising agency before looking for your first job. You could contact agencies directly to ask about placements, and make industry contacts through relevant groups on social networking sites. See the Work Experience section of the Institute of Practitioners in Advertising (IPA) website for more information and a list of member agencies. To become an advertising account executive, you will need to have good spoken and written communication skills

More information

Institute of Practitioners in Advertising (IPA)
44 Belgrave Square
London
SW1X 8QS
Tel: 020 7235 7020
www.ipa.co.uk

Account Planning Group (APG)
16 Creighton Avenue
London
N10 1NU
Tel: 020 8444 3692
www.apg.org.uk

Communication Advertising Marketing Foundation group
Tel: 01628 427120
www.camfoundation.com

Creative Skillset
Focus Point
21 Caledonian Road
London
N1 9GB
www.creativeskillset.org

Creative Skillset Careers
Tel: 08080 300 900 (England and Northern Ireland)
Tel: 0845 850 2502(Scotland)
Tel: 08000 121 815 (Wales)
www.creativeskillset.org/careers

COPYWRITERS

The nature of the work

As a copywriter, you would work as a team with an art director, who would provide the visual images to go with your words. Your job would begin with a briefing about the client, their product, the target audience and the advertising message to be put across. Your work could then involve:

- creating original ideas that fit the brief (working closely with the art director)
- presenting ideas to the agency's creative director and account team
- helping to present ideas to the client
- making any changes that the client asks for
- writing clear and persuasive copy
- making sure that ads meet the codes of advertising practice
- proofreading copy to check spelling, grammar and facts
- casting actors for TV and radio advertisements
- liaising with photographers, designers, production companies and printers.

You would often work on several projects at once, usually under the supervision of a creative director.

What can you earn?

Starting salaries can be around £18,000 to £25,000 a year. With experience this rises to between £25,000 and £50,000 a year. Senior creatives in leading agencies can earn up to £100,000 or more.

Entry requirements

Employers will usually be more interested in your creativity, writing skills and business sense than your formal qualifications.

However, advertising is a very competitive industry to join, so you may have an advantage with a qualification that includes some copywriting, such as:

- a foundation degree, BTEC HND or degree in advertising

- Communication, Advertising and Marketing Education Foundation (CAM) Diploma in Marketing Communications.
- Other useful courses include BTEC HNDs or degrees in journalism, English, media studies and marketing.

Most people get their first copywriting job as a result of work experience. This can give you the chance to make industry contacts and impress potential employers.

You could contact agencies directly to ask about placements, and make industry contacts through relevant groups on social networking sites. See the Work Experience section of the Institute of Practitioners in Advertising (IPA) website for more information and a list of member agencies. The

IPA also runs a Graduate Recruitment Agency, and D&AD runs a Graduate Placement Scheme.

When looking for jobs, you will need to show a portfolio of your work (known as a 'book') to potential employers, as you will be employed on the strength of your creative ideas, versatility and writing ability.

It's a good idea to team up with a would-be art director and work together on campaign ideas for your portfolio, as this can help prove your ability to fulfil a client's 'brief'. See D&AD's website for details of their advertising workshops, aimed at helping people build a portfolio and make contacts in the advertising industry. If you join the IPA, you can also showcase the best of your portfolio online on their All Our Best Work website. Visit the Diagonal Thinking website to find out if you have what it takes for a career in advertising.

More information

Institute of Practitioners in Advertising
44 Belgrave Square
London
SW1X 8QS
Tel: 020 7235 7020
www.ipa.co.uk

3. ARMED FORCES

Careers in the armed forces are many and varied. These will include civilian as well as non-civilian roles. In this section we look at:

- Army Officer
- Army Soldier
- Territorial Soldier
- RAF Officer
- RAF Airman or Woman
- Royal Marine
- Royal Marine Officer
- Royal Navy Officer
- Royal Navy Rating

For further information concerning the variety of jobs available in the armed forces go to:

British Army
Tel: 08457 300111
www.army.mod.uk

ARMY OFFICER

The nature of the work

The army's work can range from fighting in combat zones to providing peacekeeping duties. They can also provide disaster relief and help civil communities during difficult times, such as floods. The army officer plays an important role in the safety of the nation.

To be an army officer, you will need to have a willingness to go into combat. You need to be able to lead and motivate others. You will also need excellent teamworking skills.

To become an officer you must be aged between 17 years and 9 months and 28 years. You must pass a full army medical. You must also have at least five GCSEs and two A levels.

What can you earn?

Your pay as an army officer depends on your rank and how long you have served. Non-Graduate Officer Cadets earn around £15,300 a year while training. Graduate Officer Cadets earn £24,100 during training. Lieutenants earn between around £29,000 and £32,000 a year.

Salaries of higher ranks (from Captain to Brigadier) range from £37,200 up to £98,900 a year.

Entry requirements

To become an officer you must

- be aged between 17 years and 9 months and 28 years (upper limit could be higher depending on the role
- meet the army nationality requirement
- pass a full army medical
- have at least five GCSEs (A-C) including English, maths and a science or foreign language, plus two A levels or equivalent qualifications (180 UCAS points).

Once you show an interest in becoming an Army Officer you would be interviewed by an experienced Careers Adviser. If you show the required potential the next stage is to attend the Army Officer Selection Board (AOSB) Briefing. This is a one-and-a-half day filter selection. Successful applicants would then be invited to attend the AOSB Main Board, which is a rigorous three-day selection process that tests your physical and mental abilities and your suitability to potentially become an officer. If you pass this phase you would then be offered a place on the 44-week Commissioning Course at the Royal Military Academy Sandhurst (RMAS).

There is a separate entry process and shortened commissioning course of only four weeks for professionally qualified applicants (i.e. nurse, doctor, medical/dental officer, lawyer, veterinary surgeon or chaplain). Additional financial incentives are offered to encourage professionally qualified individuals to consider the Army as a career. For those still in education the Army offers financial incentives to progress through A levels (or attend the

Defence Sixth Form College at Welbeck), Army Scholarship Scheme, Undergraduate Cadetship or Undergraduate Bursary.

For those at university you can gain Army experience, and get paid, by joining the University Officer Training Corps. This gives a real feel for Army life but without any commitment on joining at the end of your time.

An Army Officer career is open to all applicants, but currently females cannot apply for commissions in the Household Cavalry, Royal Armoured Corps or Infantry.

More information

Wellbeck Defence Sixth Form College
Forest Road
Woodhouse
Loughborough
Leicestershire
LE12 8WD
www.dsfc.ac.uk

British Army
Tel: 08457 300111
www.army.mod.uk

ARMY SOLDIER

The nature of the work

The British army's work can range from fighting in combat zones to providing peacekeeping and humanitarian duties. If you are looking for a challenging and active job, this could be ideal for you.

To become an army soldier, you will need to have self-discipline and confidence. The Army needs people with good teamwork skills. You'll need to be able to think and react quickly in changing situations.

To join the army, you must be aged between 16 and 33. You need to meet the Army's strict nationality requirements. You must pass a full army medical examination.

What can you earn?

Your pay as a soldier in the army depends on your rank, how long you have served and the pay band for your particular job.

New recruits in training start on around £13,400 a year. On completion of 26 weeks training, this rises to over £17,000 a year.

Private soldiers can earn between £17,000 and £28,000 per year, Corporals can earn up to £35,000 a year, and those with higher ranks can earn up to around £46,000 a year.

There are additional allowances, for example whilst serving overseas, and subsidised food and accommodation. Housing for married soldiers is also subsidised to enable families to accompany their partner throughout their careers unless serving on Operations.

Entry requirements

To join the army, you must:

- be aged between 16 and 33 on the day you enlist (if you are under 18, you will need consent from a parent or guardian)
- meet the army nationality and residency requirements (see the Citizenship page of the British Army website for details)
- pass a full army medical examination.

You may need some qualifications for certain technical roles, such as in engineering or communications, but for many army jobs you will not need any. You can check the entry criteria for each job role on the British Army website, or discuss your options in detail with your local Armed Forces Careers Office. You could also take army practice tests, which aim to match you with the jobs best suited to your skills. See the British Army website for more information.

The next stage involves spending two days at your nearest Army Development and Selection Centre, which includes an interview, taking a series of physical and aptitude tests, and having a full medical examination. If you are successful, you can sign up and start the Phase One training programme. See the Training and Development section below for details.

If you are aged between 16 and 17 years and one month, you could apply for the 42-week school leavers' course at the Army Foundation College at Harrogate. See the College website for more information.

When you join the army, your contract will be for about four years. You can leave any time after this point, as long as you give 12 months' notice.

Territorial Army

You may prefer to become a part-time soldier with your local Territorial Army (TA) unit as a volunteer. You can apply to join the TA between ages 17 and 43. TA soldiers are committed to serving a minimum of 27 training days per year plus a two-week annual camp, but you can serve every weekend if you wish. Many TA soldiers choose to go on operations serving alongside regular soldiers for 6-month tours of duty. See the British Army website for details.

More information

British Army
Tel: 08457 300111
www.army.mod.uk

RAF OFFICER

The nature of the work
RAF officers are responsible for the welfare, discipline and career development of their team of non-commissioned RAF personnel (airmen and airwomen).

As an RAF officer you could choose to work in one of 20 specialist areas, each with different responsibilities, for example:

- Air Operations – pilots and weapons systems officers – flying sorties, carrying out reconnaissance, and taking part in search and rescue duties
- Operations Support – air traffic and aerospace battle managers, and flight operations officers – providing target information, coordination refuelling, digitally mapping terrain and planning missions

24

- Engineering and Logistics – aircraft and communications engineers – commissioning new aircraft, servicing fleets and managing resources and supplies
- Support Services – catering, security and training officers – providing day-to-day services for staff at RAF bases and in the field during operations
- Professions – medical, dental and nursing officers – managing specialist teams working in support of the service.

The areas of responsibility are split into squadrons and you would manage a squadron with other officers who have also earned their rank or 'commission'.

What can you earn?

New pilot officers earn £24,130 a year. Flying officers earn between £29,000 and £32,000.
Flight lieutenants can earn up to £44,200. Squadron leaders can earn around £56,000.
Salaries are independently reviewed each year, so check the latest rates with your local AFCO.

If your job involves flying, you are entitled to flying pay as well as your basic salary. If you live in RAF accommodation, a charge for rent is automatically taken from your salary.

Entry requirements

To join the RAF as an officer you must:

- be aged at least 17 years and six months
- be a UK, Republic of Ireland or Commonwealth citizen, or have dual nationality with Britain and another country
- have at least five GCSEs (A-C), including English language and - for some roles - grade B in maths, plus two A levels or similar qualifications.

For some jobs, you would need a degree or professional qualification.

Selection tests

Before you can join the RAF, you would have to pass a series of tests held at the Officers and Aircrew Selection Centre at RAF College, Cranwell in Lincolnshire. This is a three-day process that includes tests for aptitude, practical initiative and fitness, and is followed by interviews and a medical.

Scholarships and bursaries

If you are still at school or preparing to go to university, you may be eligible for an RAF sixth-form scholarship, or medical, dental or engineering sponsorship.

Check the RAF Careers website for more details about entry requirements, funding opportunities and details of your nearest Armed Forces Careers Office (AFCO).

More information

RAF Careers
Tel: 0845 605 5555
www.raf.mod.uk/careers

RAF AIRMEN AND WOMEN

The nature of the work

Royal Air Force (RAF) airmen and airwomen make up the largest number of RAF personnel. They use specialist skills in a wide range of mostly ground support roles.

As an RAF airman or airwoman, you would provide specialist support in one of the following categories:

- aircrew – which includes non-commissioned aircrew and weapon systems operators
- engineering and technical – including roles like aircraft technician
- catering and hospitality – which includes roles such as catering officer
- security and defence – with jobs in firefighting and the RAF police
- medical and medical support – dental, nursing, medical and laboratory roles
- personnel support – including administration, bands, and training

- air operations support – for example air traffic controllers
- communications and intelligence – such as photographers and intelligence analysts
- logistics and equipment – which includes drivers and supply officers.

While your exact role would vary according to your specialist skill or trade, you would also carry out military tasks like guard duties, and take part in military exercises and training.

You can contact your local Armed Forces Careers Office (AFCO) through the RAF Careers website for a full list of the trades available.

What can you earn?

Pay during training is around £13,400 a year, rising to £16,700 after training. Senior airmen/airwomen earn up to £28,400 a year. Corporals and sergeants can earn between around £25,000 and £36,200 a year.

Salaries are independently reviewed each year – check the latest rates with your local AFCO. If you are living in RAF accommodation, a charge for rent is automatically taken from your salary.

Entry requirements

Before you apply or make contact with the RAF, you should check the RAF Careers website which includes advice on exploring your options in the force.

If you decide to join the RAF as an airman or airwoman, you must be:

- at least aged 16 (upper age limits vary according to the job – check with your local AFCO and the RAF Careers website)
- a citizen of the UK, Republic of Ireland or the Commonwealth, or have dual nationality with Britain and another country.

You will also need to pass a series of tests, covering:

- aptitude
- practical initiative
- health and fitness.

You would then be interviewed and have a medical assessment.

Tests usually take place at an AFCO. For some of the trades you will need GCSEs and BTEC or City & Guilds qualifications.

Most trades are open to men and women. However, women are not able to join the RAF Regiment, which involves combat. For more details on all requirements, check the RAF Careers website.

More information

RAF Careers
Tel: 0845 605 5555
www.raf.mod.uk/careers

ROYAL MARINES COMMANDO

The nature of the work
Royal Marines are part of the Royal Navy. They take part in front-line combat (on land and at sea) and are sent at short notice to deal with emergency situations, which may include military operations or natural disasters. If you are physically fit, resourceful and have self-discipline, this could be for you.

In this job you will need to be resilient and determined. You will need to follow orders. You will also need to think and react quickly under pressure.

To become a Royal Marines commando you must be male and a British citizen. You do not need any formal qualifications, however, you must pass the Royal Navy selection process.

What can you earn?

On entry, Royal Marines earn around £13,337 a year. This can rise to between £16,681 and £28,372 a year. Non-Commissioned Officers (corporals and sergeants) can earn around £32,000 to £36,200. Senior Non-Commissioned Officers (colour sergeants and warrant officers) can earn up to £45,800.

Extra allowances may be paid for family separation and special service. All medical and dental care is free. Where housing is provided, deductions may be made from the monthly income.

Entry requirements

As a first step to joining the Royal Marines you should visit your local armed forces careers office (AFCO), where you will be able to pick up free leaflets and have an informal chat about your career options. You can search for your local AFCO on the Army Jobs website.

To become a Royal Marines commando you must be male and a British citizen. You do not need any formal qualifications, however, you must pass the Royal Navy selection process. This involves:

- aptitude tests for reasoning, English language, numeracy and mechanical comprehension
  an interview and medical check
- a pre-joining fitness test, including two 2.4km runs on a treadmill, to be completed within 12 minutes 30 seconds and 10 minutes 30 seconds respectively
- the Potential Royal Marine Course (PRMC), which lasts three days and includes physical tests, classroom-based work and an interview.

As a commando you will serve an open engagement which lasts for 18 years (this can be extended up to the age of 55). You will usually be able to hand in 12 months' notice if you wish to leave after serving a minimum of three years.

See the Royal Navy website for more information and a list of specialist areas of work.

More information

Ryal navy
Careers Enquiries: 0845 607 5555
www.royalnavy.mod.uk

Armed Forces Careers Office (NI)
Royal Navy and Royal Marines
Palace Barracks
Holywood
Co Down
BT18 9RA
Tel: 028 9042 7040

ROYAL MARINES OFFICER

The nature of the work

Royal Marines (RM) officers lead teams of commando-trained soldiers in combat situations, at sea or on shore. Increasingly, RM officers are involved in leading peace-keeping and humanitarian missions.

As an RM officer, you would be responsible for the day-to-day welfare and discipline of the marines under your command. You would usually start out as a troop officer in charge of 28 men. Your duties would involve leading the troop and making decisions about their training and deployment.

What can you earn?

Trainees can earn between £15,300 and £24,150 a year. Captains earn between £36,160 and £43,000. Colonels can earn up to £85,300.

Extra allowances may be paid, for example when overseas or on flying duties. Deductions may be made where accommodation is provided.

Entry requirements

To apply for Royal Marine officer training, you will need:

- a minimum height of 1.51 metres and weight in proportion to your height
- to pass a medical assessment
- to meet the Royal Marines nationality and residence requirement
- to be at least age 17 (upper age limits vary depending on your specialism)
- a minimum of five GCSEs (A-C) including English and maths, plus two A levels (alternative qualifications may also be accepted).

If you have a UK degree you can apply for marine officer training through direct graduate entry. Financial support through scholarships, sponsorships and bursaries is sometimes available to help with sixth-form and degree-level study. Check with your Armed Forces Careers Office for full details of all criteria.

You must also pass a three-day Potential Officers Course, which will test your physical ability, endurance, mental aptitude and leadership skills. This is followed by an interview.

You will join the service as an officer on a 12-year Initial Commission. You would usually need to serve a minimum of between three and five years.

More information

Royal Navy
Careers Enquiries: 0845 607 5555
www.royal-navy.mod.uk

Armed Forces Careers Office (NI)
Royal Navy and Royal Marines
Palace Barracks
Holywood
Co Down
BT18 9RA
Tel: 028 9042 7040

ROYAL NAVY OFFICER

The nature of the work
Royal Navy officers are senior managers in the Royal Navy, working onboard ships and submarines.

As an officer, you would be responsible for the welfare and management of those serving in your squadron or unit. You would also have a specialist role such as:

- warfare officer – controlling weapons and defence systems, and assisting with navigation
- air engineering officer – making the ship's aircraft ready to fly when needed, and working with industry to improve aircraft design
- weapons engineering officer – overseeing the maintenance of weapons delivery systems, detection sensors, and communications equipment
- logistics officer – managing the delivery of supplies and equipment, and giving advice on the legal and financial implications
- medical or nursing officer – providing medical care on ships, submarines and ashore.

31

For details on the full range of officer specialisms, see the Royal Navy website.

What can you earn?

Lieutenants earn from £37,915 to £45,090 a year. Lieutenant commanders earn from £47,760 to £57,199. Commanders earn between £67,031 and £77,617. Captains can earn up to £89,408.

Deductions may be made if accommodation is provided. Extra allowances are paid for family separation, special service and flying duties.

Entry requirements

To get on to Royal Navy officer training, you will need:

- to be at least age 17 (the upper age limit varies according to the specialism)
- a minimum height of 151.5cm
- to meet strict eyesight standards
- to pass a medical
- to meet the Royal Navy nationality and residence requirements.

You will also need qualifications equivalent to:

- five GCSEs (A-C), including English and Maths
  two A levels.
- If you have a degree you could apply through Direct Graduate Entry.

Check with your local Armed Forces Careers Office (listed on the Royal Navy Careers website) for a full explanation of all criteria.

Financial support through scholarships and bursaries is sometimes available to help with sixth-form and degree-level study; see the Royal Navy Careers website for details.

For all officer roles you need to pass the Admiralty Interview Board at HMS Sultan in Hampshire. This is a two-day assessment which includes interviews and tests in communication, maths, mental agility, spatial orientation and physical fitness.

You can get full information and advice on Royal Navy officer careers by ringing the Royal Navy Career Enquiries helpline.

More information

Royal Navy
Careers Enquiries: 0845 607 5555
www.royal-navy.mod.uk

Armed Forces Careers Office (NI)
Royal Navy and Royal Marines
Palace Barracks
Holywood
Co Down
BT18 9RA
Tel: 028 9042 7040

ROYAL NAVY RATING

The nature of the work
Royal Navy ratings work in a variety of job roles onboard ships or submarines at sea, or in a Royal Navy shore base.

As a royal navy rating, your work will vary depending on which branch of the service you support and your specific trade. Branches and related duties include:

- warfare – operating and maintaining the ship's weapons, electronic systems and sensors; co-ordinating the ship's communications systems
- engineering – operating, maintaining and refitting the Royal Navy's ships, submarines and aircraft
- logistics – operating and co-ordinating a range of office, accounting, stores and catering systems
- naval air branch – ensuring that Navy aircraft are prepared for action and giving navigation information based on weather and ocean conditions
- submarine service – operating and maintaining a submarine's weapons, electronic systems and sensors.

What can you earn?

Starting salaries are from £13,895 a year. Able ratings can earn between £17,265 and £28,939 a year. Warrant officers can earn up to £46,753 a year.

Submariners, divers and anyone required to fly, may receive additional pay. Extra allowances are also paid for family separations. Where accommodation is provided, deductions may be made from monthly pay.

Entry requirements

To join the Royal Navy you will need to pass a selection test, interview and medical examination. For many jobs or trades within the Navy, there are no formal academic entry requirements and you will receive training on the job. However, you will have a wider choice of careers if you have some GCSEs (A-C). Your local Royal Navy Careers Office can advise you further on your options, and the exact requirements.

- Entry to the Royal Navy is possible from the age of 16 for most trades. The exceptions are:
- medical assistants, dental surgery assistants and dental hygienists (17)
- divers (18)
- student naval nurses (17 years, 6 months)
- direct entry registered general nurses (21).

For all trades, the upper age limit at entry is 36. The upper age limit may be waived for exceptional candidates. You will need to apply at least six months in advance of the age limit.

The minimum height for all entrants is 151.5 centimetres and your weight must be in proportion to your height. There are strict eyesight standards and, for some jobs, normal colour vision is essential. You must also meet nationality and residence requirements.

More information

Royal Navy
Careers Enquiries: 0845 607 5555
www.royal-navy.mod.uk

Armed Forces Careers Office (NI)
Royal Navy and Royal Marines
Palace Barracks
Holywood Co Down BT18 9RA
Tel: 028 9042 7040

****

4. BANKING AND FINANCE

Like accountancy, banking is a very diverse industry. Bankers have come to the forefront since the onset of the credit crunch and not in a favourable way. However, you should ignore the negative publicity as banking is a very worthwhile and rewarding career.

There are several different types of bank. Firstly, there are the traditional retail banks which are high street banks with branches across the country, these are the banks that most people deal with on a day to day basis. Then there are the investment banks dealing with large companies and other investment organisations.

There are many different types of role in the banking world, ranging from cashiers through to more senior roles such as bank managers and brokers.

In this section, we look at:

- Cashiers and Customer Services Advisors
- Bank Management
- Building Society Jobs
- Commodity Brokers
- Financial Advisors

CASHIERS OR CUSTOMER SERVICE ADVISORS

The nature of the work
The above deal with all general queries, made in person or by phone or in writing or via the web. They will, typically, work in either branches or call centres. They will be responsible for a wide variety of functions, such as processing cash and cheques and dealing with foreign currency. Senior cashiers will work in a supervisory role. All in all, those who enter the world of banking via a cashier role will gain valuable experience of work at the ground floor, experience that will stand them in good stead for more senior roles later on.

Entry requirements

Banks will set their own entry requirements but most will set entry tests which will assess the level of maths, English and IT skills. These are the most important attributes which will help a candidate gain entry to the world of banking. Most banks will require GCSE grades A-C. Once having gained entry training is on the job. Training to a higher level is provided to enable candidates to progress to manager level.

BANK MANAGER

The role of the bank manager is rather more complex. The manager will be involved in strategic planning and they will usually be placed in a branch, being responsible for the running of a branch. The manager will be involved also in putting together sales strategies and offering advice to clients.

Entry to management level

There are two main routes into management-as mentioned above through promotion from cashier/customer services advisor or buy joining a training scheme run by the bank. Most banks will expect a good honours degree in a business or finance related subject, but some will accept good A levels.

Managers will normally work towards a professional qualification, including The Professional Diploma in Financial Services Management, The Applied Diploma in Corporate Banking and the Applied Diploma in Retailing Financial Services. Banks will also run their own management courses in house as the job progresses.

What can you earn?

Cashiers will start on a salary of between 14,000-16,500 which will rise with experience. Managers will usually start on 21,000-25,000 which again rises with experience. Many roles will incorporate bonuses although these have now been moderated following the general and ongoing furore over bankers pay.

More information

British Bankers Association (BBA)
020 7216 8000
www.bba.org.uk

37

Financial Services Skills Council
0845 257 3772
www.fssc.org.uk

BUILDING SOCIETY JOBS

Although building societies are structured differently to banks, in terms of their legal structure, the jobs available largely mirror those within banks. For more information concerning jobs in building societies contact:

Building Societies Association
020 7520 5900
www.bsa.org.uk

Outside of the banks, there are other important and rewarding roles, such as:

COMMODITY BROKERS

The nature of the work
Commodity brokers buy and sell a variety of commodities , which will include grain, coffee, oil, gas and metals. In addition to trading actual products they will also deal in what are known as futures, which are commodities that will be produced in the future. Prices are fixed way into the future and gains or losses can be made. There is an element of risk involved here. Commodity brokers will work in conjunction with a variety of organisations such as transport, shipping and insurance.

Entry requirements
Most successful applicants in this field will be highly numerate and have a good degree in a relevant subject such as economics or maths. Applicants can earn high salaries, with new entrants earning between 35,000 to 50,000. Experienced brokers can earn many times this amount.

More information
Financial Services Skills Council
0845 257 3772

www.fssc.org.uk
Intercontinental Exchange
020 7481 0643
www.theice.com

The London Metal Exchange
020 7264 5555
www.lme.co.uk

FINANCIAL ADVISORS

Financial advisers help their clients choose financial products and services. These might be investments, savings or pensions. They can also be mortgages and insurance. If you are interested in finance and you want to help people make decisions, this could be an ideal job for you.

A financial adviser needs to be able to explain complex information clearly and simply. They need to have good maths and computer skills. They also need to be trustworthy.

The nature of the work
As a financial adviser, your work would normally involve:
- having meetings with clients
- talking to clients about their current finances and future plans
- researching financial products
- explaining details of products so that clients can make informed choices
- preparing clear recommendations
- meeting performance and sales targets
- negotiating with providers of financial products
- keeping detailed records
- dealing with client enquiries
- producing financial reports
- keeping clients regularly updated about their investments
- keeping up to date with new products and changes in the law.

You could work as a 'tied', 'multi-tied' or independent financial adviser:

- tied – usually working for banks, building societies or insurance companies, and only offering your own company's financial products
- multi-tied – dealing with a number of companies and only selling products from those companies
- independent financial adviser (IFA) – offering products and giving advice on all financial products on the market.

You would need to follow strict financial industry rules and guidelines. These make sure that you act fairly and that you are properly qualified to give appropriate financial advice.

What can you earn?

Financial advisers working for a company are usually paid a basic salary plus commission. Independent financial advisers can be paid either a fee or commission. Basic salaries without commission for trainee and newly qualified advisers can be around £22,000 to £30,000 a year. As an experienced financial adviser, you may earn up to £40,000 a year. Successful advisers, especially those working in wealth management or private client advice, may earn between £50,000 and £70,000 or more a year, with commission.

Entry requirements

You could become a financial adviser with various qualifications and experience. Many employers consider 'people skills' and a strong background in customer service, sales or financial services to be more important than formal qualifications.

A common way to start this career is as a tied adviser in a bank, building society or insurance company. You would do this job after being promoted from a customer service role and achieving an industry-regulated qualification. These qualifications are known as 'appropriate qualifications'. See the Financial Skills Partnership (FSP) website for details.

You could also start as a paraplanner – a person who provides administrative support and research for independent financial advisers. If you are not already working in financial services, you could take an approved qualification for trainee financial advisers before you join the industry. See the Training and Development section below for details.

Some banks, building societies and large firms of independent financial advisers (IFAs) offer graduate training schemes for new advisers who have degrees or similar qualifications.

You may be able to start this career through a Level 4 Higher Apprenticeship in providing financial advice. You will need to check if there are schemes available in your area. For more information, visit the Apprenticeships or FSP websites.

More information
Financial Skills Partnership
51 Gresham Street
London
EC2V 7HQ
Tel: 0845 257 3772
www.financialskillspartnership.org.uk

Chartered Insurance Institute
42-48 High Road
South Woodford
London
E18 2JP
Tel: 020 8989 8464
www.discoverrisk.co.uk
www.cii.co.uk

Personal Finance Society
42-48 High Road
South Woodford
London
E18 2JP
Tel: 020 8530 0852
www.thepfs.org

5. CATERING

Catering is a diverse profession, with many opportunities on offer. In this section we look at the roles of:

- Catering Manager
- Chef
- Food Scientist
- Consumer Scientist
- Baker

For details of other jobs within the industry go to:

People first
2nd Floor
Armstrong House
38 Market Square
Uxbridge
Middlesex
UB8 1LH
Tel: 01895 817 000
www.people1st.co.uk

CATERING MANAGER

The nature of the work

As a catering manager, you could work in hotels, small independent restaurants, eateries that are part of a large chain, and fast food outlets. Your role would be to make sure that the restaurant runs smoothly, overseeing the business side as well as ensuring high standards for customers.

As a catering manager you would work in larger catering operations, such as business or factory canteens, hospitals or schools. You would have less contact with customers than a restaurant manager, and spend more time behind the scenes.

Your duties as a restaurant or catering manager would include:

- planning menus
- advertising vacancies and recruiting staff
- making sure that all staff are fully trained
- keeping staff motivated to provide the highest standard of service
- organising shifts and rotas
- managing stock control and budgets
- running the business in line with strict hygiene, health and safety guidelines.

What can you earn?

Entry requirements

To apply for a trainee manager job, you will usually need a good standard of general education plus relevant experience.

You could work your way up to a management position, for example by starting as a waiter/waitress. With experience and qualifications you could take on more responsibilities and supervise less experienced colleagues. You could then apply for a head of waiting staff or assistant manager post. Qualifications include:

- Level 2 NVQ Diploma in Food and Beverage Service
- Level 3 Advanced Apprenticeship in Hospitality & Catering (Supervision & Leadership).

Many large restaurants, fast food chains and catering companies run management trainee schemes that can lead to management roles. You would usually need a qualification such as a foundation degree, BTEC HNC/HND or degree, or relevant experience, in order to be accepted on a scheme.

More information

Springboard UK
Http://springboarduk.net

People first
2nd Floor
Armstrong House
38 Market Square
Uxbridge
Middlesex
UB8 1LH
Tel: 01895 817 000
www.people1st.co.uk

UKSP
www.uksp.co.uk

CHEF

The nature of the work

Chefs prepare food using a variety of cooking methods. In large kitchens they normally work as part of a team, and look after one food area, like bread and pastries, or vegetables. The head chef (also known as executive chef, kitchen manager or chef de cuisine) runs the entire kitchen.

Your main tasks as a chef would include:

- preparing, cooking and presenting food in line with required standards
- keeping preparation at the right level
- making sure that food is served promptly
- monitoring food production to ensure consistent quality and portion size
- stock control

44

- following relevant hygiene, health and safety guidelines.

You would usually start as a kitchen assistant or trainee chef (also known as commis chef). At this level you would spend time in each area of the kitchen, learning a range of skills and how to look after kitchen equipment.

With experience, you could progress to section chef (also known as station chef and chef de partie), where you would be in charge of an area of the kitchen. The next step would be sous chef, where you would be running the entire kitchen for the head chef when needed. At head chef level, you would be responsible for creating and updating the menus, and for producing and meeting financial budgets.

What can you earn?

A trainee (commis) chef may start on a salary of around £12,200 a year. Section chefs (chefs de partie) can earn up to £16,000 a year, and a second chef (sous chef) may earn around £22,000 a year.

Head chefs (chefs de cuisine) can earn up to £30,000 a year. An executive head chef in a top hotel can earn between £40,000 and £50,000.

Entry requirements

You may not need any academic qualifications to start work as a trainee (commis) chef. However, some employers will prefer you to have a good general standard of education, possibly including a hospitality or catering qualification.

Another way to prepare for this work would be to take one of the following qualifications. Some of these also combine classroom study with practical experience and work placements:

- Level 1 Diploma in Introduction to Professional Cookery/Level 2 Diploma in Professional Cookery
- Level 1 NVQ Certificate in Food Production and Cooking/Level 2 NVQ Diploma in Food Production and Cooking
- Level 2 NVQ Diploma in Professional Cookery

45

- Level 2 Certificate in Hospitality and Catering Principles (Professional Cookery) or (Food Production and Cooking).

Check with colleges for details of course entry requirements.

Another option is to progress as a chef through a Level 2 Apprenticeship in Hospitality and Catering (Food Production & Cooking) or (Professional Cookery). You will need to check which schemes are available in your area. To find out more about Apprenticeships in hospitality, visit the Apprenticeships and UKSP websites.

More information

Springboard UK
http://springboarduk.net

People first
2nd Floor
Armstrong House
38 Market Square
Uxbridge
Middlesex
UB8 1LH
Tel: 01895 817 000
www.people1st.co.uk

FOOD SCIENTIST/TECHNOLOGIST

The nature of the work
As a food scientist, you would use scientific techniques to:

- provide accurate nutritional information for food labelling
- investigate ways to keep food fresh, safe and attractive
- find ways of producing food more quickly and cheaply
- test the safety and quality of food.

As a food technologist, you would plan the manufacture of food and drink products and your duties may include:

- working on newly discovered ingredients to invent new recipes and ideas
- modifying foods, for example creating fat-free products
- conducting experiments and producing sample products
- designing the processes and machinery for making products in large quantities.

Some jobs (for example carrying out research for a supermarket chain) may involve quality control as well as product development.

As a food scientist or food technologist you would also gain knowledge and experience of areas like chemical engineering, production planning, market and consumer research, and financial management.

What can you earn?
Starting salaries for food scientists and technologists can be between £20,000 and £25,000 a year. With experience and increased responsibilities, this can rise to between £30,000 and £45,000.

Entry requirements
You will need a strong background in science, usually through a BTEC HNC/HND or degree in a subject such as food science, food studies, or food technology.

To get on to a degree you will usually need:

- five GCSEs (A-C), and
- two or three A levels, preferably in chemistry or biology.

For a BTEC HNC/HND, entry requirements are usually one or two A levels or equivalent.

You can search for courses on the Universities and Colleges Admissions Service (UCAS) website, and you should check directly with course providers for exact requirements.

If you have a degree in an unrelated subject, you could improve your chances of employment by taking a postgraduate course in a subject such as food safety or food quality management.

Visit the Institute of Food Science and Technology careers website for more information including details of relevant courses.

Alternatively, you could begin as a lab technician and work towards further qualifications whilst in employment. For this level you would need at least four GCSEs (A-C) including English, maths, and a science subject. See the laboratory technician job profile for more information.

Another option could be to enter through an apprenticeship scheme. The range of Apprenticeships available in your area will depend on the local jobs market and the types of skills employers need from their workers. The most suitable Apprenticeship in Food and Drink (Food Industry Skills). To find out more, visit the Apprenticeships website.

More information

Improve Ltd
Providence House
2 Innovation Close
York
YO10 5ZF
Tel: 0845 644 0448
www.improveltd.co.uk

Institute of Food Science and Technology (IFST)
5 Cambridge Court
210 Shepherd's Bush Road
London
W6 7NJ
Tel: 020 7603 6316
www.ifst.org

IFST Careers
www.foodtechcareers.org

Chartered Institute of Environmental Health
Chadwick Court
15 Hatfields
London
SE1 8DJ
Tel: 020 7928 6006
www.cieh.org

CIEH Careers Website
www.ehcareers.org

The Food and Drink Federation
6 Catherine Street
London
WC2B 5JJ
Tel: 020 7836 2460
www.fdf.org.uk

CONSUMER SCIENTIST

The nature of the work

As a consumer scientist, you would provide a key link between consumers and manufacturers. Your work would involve:

- researching the tastes, needs, aspirations and preferences of consumers
- giving advice (for example to retailers) on how to improve the quality, design, production, delivery and popularity of an item or service.

You could use your knowledge of consumer behaviour in a variety of industries. For example in food product development, you would work with a supermarket chain or manufacturer, researching and designing new dishes to attract consumers.

Other areas you could be involved with include:

- marketing – using market research to help marketing professionals develop, package, advertise and distribute a product or campaign
- quality assurance – developing tests to make sure products meet quality standards and legal requirements
- consumer advice – representing consumers' rights, using knowledge of relevant legislation
- catering – advising hotels, restaurants, schools, residential care homes or hospitals on the type of food to provide
- product and service development – advising on products ranging from household goods to public amenities
- publishing and public relations – producing information on cookery, family health and new products, or liaising with the media
- education – advising on healthy living, in schools or further and higher education
- government departments – working for bodies such as the Food Standards Agency or Trading Standards to enforce food safety and consumer protection laws.

Your main duties are likely to involve researching and writing reports, carrying out experiments (for example, developing recipes), recruiting and training panels or focus groups, and conducting interviews with consumers.

What can you earn?

- Starting salaries can be between £17,000 and £22,500 a year.
- With experience, earnings can rise to around £30,000.
- Managers may earn around £40,000 to £50,000.

Entry requirements

Many employers will want you to have a degree or BTEC HND in a subject such as:

- consumer studies
- consumer product management
- food and consumer management
- food science or technology
- psychology

- marketing
- statistics.

To get on to a degree you will usually need five GCSEs (A-C) and two A levels. However, you should check with course providers because alternative qualifications may also be accepted. Some employers may prefer you to have a postgraduate qualification, for instance in behavioural psychology or consumer behaviour. Experience in food manufacturing or market research could be an advantage or an alternative way of getting into consumer science.

More information

Improve Ltd
Providence House
2 Innovation Close
York
YO10 5ZF
Tel: 0845 644 0448
http://www.improve-skills.co.uk/
www.improveltd.co.uk

Food Standards Agency
Aviation House
125 Kingsway
London
WC2B 6NH
Tel: 020 7276 8000
www.foodstandards.gov.uk

BAKER

The nature of the work
At a plant bakery, you would use machinery and production lines to manufacture large amounts of baked goods for shops, supermarkets and other large customers.

As an in-store baker, for example with a supermarket, you would use some automated machinery to make fresh bread products to be sold in the store.

At a craft bakery, you would create a smaller amount of products to be sold in a shop, delicatessen or chain of specialist shops. This work would be more varied, and although some machinery is used, you would do much of the work by hand.

What can you earn?

Bakers can earn between £11,600 and £16,000 a year. With experience, specialist skills or supervisory responsibilities, this could rise to around £20,000 to £25,000 a year. Additional payments may be made for working overtime or shifts.

Entry requirements

You can apply for work as a trainee in a bakery without any specific qualifications. However, having GCSEs in English, maths, science or food technology could help you.

You could learn bakery skills and develop your knowledge through part-time and full-time courses at further education colleges. Qualifications you could gain include:

- Level 2 Certificate/Diploma in Professional Bakery
- Level 3 Diploma in Professional Bakery
- Level 3 Diploma in Professional Bakery, Science and Technology.

You may be able to do this job through an Apprenticeship scheme. The most suitable Apprenticeship is the Improve Proficiency Apprenticeship in Food and Drink (Bakery Industry Skills). You will need to check which schemes are available in your area. To find out more, see the Apprenticeships website.

More information

Improve Ltd
Providence House

2 Innovation Close
York
YO10 5ZF
Tel: 0845 644 0448
www.improveltd.co.uk

Federation of Bakers
6 Catherine Street
London
WC2B 5JW
Tel: 020 7420 7190
www.bakersfederation.org.uk

****

6. CIVIL SERVICE AND LOCAL GOVERNMENT

The civil service is vast and forms the backbone of government. There are numerous opportunities within the civil service, many of them concentrated in London but also many in various departments in the UK as a whole from local government to administration of passports and driving licences. In this section we look at:

- Civil Service Administrative Officer
- Civil Service Executive Officer
- Diplomatic Services Officer
- Local Government Administrative assistant
- Town Planning Support Staff
- Registrar of Births, Deaths and marriages and Civil Partnerships

For further information about the variety of jobs in the civil service you should go to www.civilservice.gov.uk

CIVIL SERVICE ADMINISTRATION OFFICER

The nature of the work
Your main tasks at administrative officer (AO) or administrative assistant (AA) grade would be to deal with customers, update records and carry out routine clerical duties. Your day-to-day work would depend on which department or agency you worked for, but might include:

- handling enquiries from the public in person, by telephone or by letter
- updating computerised and paper-based records
- processing benefit payments
- researching information
- filing, photocopying and other administrative tasks.

With experience, you could deal with more complex enquiries or complaints, or take on more specialist work related to your department.

What can you earn?

Administrative assistants start on around £12,000 a year. Administrative officers start on around £14,500 a year. With experience and good performance this can rise to between £16,000 and £20,000 a year.

Entry requirements

Each department and agency organises its own recruitment and sets its own entry requirements.

You do not need formal qualifications for many jobs. Instead, you would take an aptitude test to prove your ability in areas like teamwork, communication and number skills. However, some departments may ask for five GCSEs (A-C) or similar qualifications for certain jobs.

You must also meet the nationality requirement. All jobs are open to British nationals and around 75% are also open to Commonwealth citizens or European Union nationals. See the Civil Service website for more information.

More information

There aren't any central telephone number for information - see the Civil Service Website for contacts for individual departments.

CIVIL SERVICE EXECUTIVE OFFICER

The nature of the work

Executive officers are the first level of management in the civil service. As an executive officer, you could work in any of the 170 civil service departments and agencies that deal with developing policies and delivering services to the public. All departments and agencies employ people at executive officer (EO) grade, although job titles can vary widely.

Your exact duties would depend on the department you worked for, but could include:

- managing a team of administrative officers being responsible for motivating, training and appraising team members
- training in a specific area of work such as tax or immigration control
- handling a caseloads

- applying complex laws and procedures to deal with problems and enquiries
- using computer systems and databases
- preparing and presenting reports.

What can you earn?

Salaries at EO grade are between around £21,000 and £24,000 a year. Salaries are higher in London. There may be extra allowances for working unsocial hours.

Entry requirements

You could join a civil service department in an administrative grade and work your way up, or you could be recruited directly as an executive officer.

Each department organises its own recruitment and sets its own entry requirements. You may need two A levels or equivalent qualifications for some jobs at EO grade, but in many cases you will not be asked for any formal qualifications. Instead, when you apply you would go through various stages, which might include:

- filling in an application form based on your skills and life experience
- taking a written test to check your level of English and maths
- passing more selection tests and an interview.

If you have a first or second class honours degree, you can apply to the Fast Stream Development Programme. This is a four-year training scheme that leads to senior management posts. Your degree can be in any subject, although some departments may prefer degrees in subjects that are relevant to their work.

Competition for places on the Fast Stream is very strong, and you must pass a series of selection tests and interviews. Fast Stream is usually only open to UK nationals. See the Civil Service website for more information on the Fast Stream.

For all jobs you must also meet the nationality requirement – all jobs are open to British nationals and around 75% are also open to Commonwealth citizens or European Union nationals. You can find more information on the Civil Service website.

More information

No central telephone number for information, see Civil Service Jobs Online for contacts for individual departments.

DIPLOMATIC SERVICE OFFICER

The nature of the work

The work of the FCO is very varied and covers every area where British interests and citizens are involved internationally, for example:

- political – monitoring political and economic developments in the host country, and representing Britain to that country's government and media
- commercial – helping British companies to trade in the host country, and promoting investment into Britain
- consular – helping British citizens in the host country, and processing visa applications from local people who wish to come to Britain.

Your day-to-day duties would depend on your grade. For example:

- Policy Officers (grade C4) – researching issues and helping to develop policy and strategy
- Executive Assistants (A2) – drafting letters, handling accounts and invoices, and providing clerical support
- Administrative Assistants (A1) – providing clerical support.

As a UK-based Policy or Operational Officer, you might be responsible for one country or geographical area, or for a specific foreign policy issue that affects many countries.

What can you earn?

Administrative Assistants start on £16,635 a year (plus London allowance where appropriate). Executive assistants start on £18,885 a year. Operational Officers start on £21,432. Policy (Fast Stream) Officers start on £26,102 a year. All London-based staff are also awarded an extra allowance of £3,000 a year for when working in London. Staff working overseas may be paid additional allowances.

Entry requirements

The qualifications and experience that you need to join the Foreign and Commonwealth Office will vary depending on the grade of job you are applying for.

To join as a C4 Policy Entrant through the civil service's Fast Stream programme, you must have at least a second class degree in any subject. You must then pass a series of skills-based online and practical tests. See the Faststream website for more information on the Fast Stream recruitment process.

For Executive Assistant (A2) posts you will need at least five GCSEs (A-C) including English and maths, or equivalent qualifications. For Administrative Assistant (A1) posts you will need two GCSEs (A-C) including English, or equivalent.

To join the FCO at any grade, you must meet the nationality and residency requirements, and pass a strict security vetting process. See the Careers section of the FCO website for full details of these.

Each job's selection process involves several stages, and can take several months to complete especially at the higher grades.

For the policy grade, previous work experience in management, business or public administration would be useful, though not essential.

You will find it useful to have experience of office work for the administrative grades, and your typing skills will be tested during the selection process.

More information

Foreign and Commonwaelth Office
www.fco.gov.uk

Civil Service Jobs Online
No central telephone number for information, see website for contacts for

individual departments
www.civilservice.gov.uk

Careers in operational delivery- helps you to explore the different career pathways you would need to follow to get to specific job roles within Operational Delivery

www.civilservice.gov.uk/my-civil-service/networks/professional/operational-delivery/leading-opdel-profession.aspx

---

LOCAL GOVERNMENT ADMINISTRATIVE ASSISTANT

The nature of the work
You could work in any local authority department, for example housing, social services, education or planning.

Your duties would vary according to the department you worked in, but they might include:

- dealing with enquiries by phone, in writing or in person
- looking up information on a computer system
- filing and photocopying
- producing and sending letters
- sorting, recording and distributing mail
- dealing with cash and payments
- updating computerised and clerical records
- acting as a secretary or personal assistant (PA) to a manager or department
- liaising with staff in other departments.
- You may also be known by a number of different job titles such as administrative officer, clerical officer, customer service assistant, or support officer.

What can you earn?
Salaries are usually between £13,000 and £19,000 a year, depending on experience and responsibilities.

Entry requirements

For most jobs, you will need a good standard of general education, and good computer or keyboard skills. You will usually find it useful to have experience of customer service or office work.

Although you may have an advantage with some GCSEs including maths and English, many councils do not ask for formal qualifications. Instead, they will test you in the skills you need for the job, for example communication, IT and ability with numbers.

You should check with individual councils about the exact qualifications and experience needed for each job.

You may be able to get into this job through an Apprenticeship scheme. The range of Apprenticeships available in your area will depend on the local jobs market and the types of skills employers need from their workers. To find out more, visit the Apprenticeships website.

More information

LG careers
www.lgcareers.com

Skills CFA
6 Graphite Square
Vauxhall Walk
London
SE11 5EE
Tel: 020 7091 9620
www.cfa.uk.com

LOCAL GOVERNMENT OFFICER

The nature of the work
You could work in a variety of departments and roles, such as planning council services in a policy section, or delivering services in a department like education or housing. Job titles at this level could include best value officer, external funding officer, policy officer and democratic services officer.

Your day-to-day tasks would vary according to the department and your level of responsibility. They may include:

- managing and evaluating projects
- writing reports and briefing papers
- dealing with enquiries and giving advice
- presenting information at meetings
- supervising administrative work and managing clerical staff
- keeping records
- preparing and managing contracts
- liaising with other agencies
- managing budgets and funding.

What can you earn?

Starting salaries can be between £16,000 and £20,000 a year, depending on the job. With experience this can rise to between £22,000 and £38,000.

Entry requirements

The skills and experience that are needed will vary depending on the duties and level of responsibility, so you should check the entry requirements carefully for each job. For some jobs, employers will ask for qualifications to degree standard, or equivalent work experience. Most councils value life experience and may accept you without the exact qualifications that they have asked for, as long as you have enough relevant experience and the skills needed for the job.

If you have a good degree in any subject, you may be able to join many local authorities in England and Wales through the National Graduate Development Programme. Some other local authorities run their own graduate or management training schemes for new entrants. See the National Graduate Development Programme website for more information.

More information

LG Careers
www.lgcareers.com

Institute of Chattered Secretaries and Administrators (ICSA)
16 Park Crescent

London
W1B 1AH
Tel: 020 7580 4741
www.icsa.org.uk

Institute of Administrative Management
Caroline House
55-57 High Holborn
London
WC1V 6DX
Tel: 020 7841 1100
www.instam.org

TOWN PLANNING SUPPORT STAFF

The nature of the work

Town planning support staff help to process planning applications submitted by individuals and businesses. This is a broad role that includes everything from giving advice to the public, to technical planning and office duties.

- As a support staff member, your responsibilities would include:
- preparing reports for internal and external publications
- recording minutes at meetings
- building and managing technical libraries, filing systems and databases
- drawing up designs, using computer-aided design (CAD) software
- carrying out data surveys, for example traffic impact assessments
- supplying information and data to planners for applications
- recording the progress and outcomes of planning applications
- organising public meetings
- answering enquiries about application procedures.

You might also work in planning enforcement, which would involve:

- working with individuals and businesses to make sure that they comply with the conditions set out in their application decisions
- gathering information to use as evidence in disputes

- presenting reports on breaches to planning committees or, where necessary, to magistrates and judges.

You would usually work for a local authority, independent planning consultancy, government department or a private company, for example a property developer.

What can you earn?

Starting salaries are between £14,000 and £18,000 a year. Experienced staff can earn between £18,500 and £23,000. Qualified technical staff with supervisory duties can earn up to £28,000.

Entry requirements

Most employers will expect you to have GCSEs or A levels, in relevant subjects such as maths, English, geography, IT or economics, or equivalent qualifications.

Specific qualifications and/or experience in surveying, CAD design, construction, information management, administration or law may also be useful skills for getting into this career.

See the Royal Town Planning Institute (RTPI) website for more details about careers in this field, and the Local Government careers website for information about local government planning.

More information

Royal Town Planning Institute
41 Botolph Lane
London
EC3R 8DL
Tel: 020 7929 9494
www.rtpi.org.uk

LG Jobs
www.lgcareers.com

REGISTRAR OF BIRTHS MARRIAGES AND CIVIL PARTNERSHIPS

The nature of the work

In this job your main duties would include:

- interviewing parents and relatives after a birth or a death
- completing computerised and paper records
- issuing birth or death certificates
- informing the coroner (or procurator fiscal in Scotland) if there are any suspicious circumstances surrounding a death
- collecting statistics to send to the General Register Office
- taking payment for copies of certificates
- keeping accurate records
- performing civil ceremonies.

You could also be employed as a celebrant, conducting civil ceremonies such as marriages, civil partnerships and civil funerals without the responsibility of registering births and deaths. You could be employed by a local council, or you could work independently (see the Association of Independent Celebrants for information). If you share humanist beliefs, you could also become an officiant or celebrant of the British Humanist Association.

What can you earn?

Assistant registrars usually start on around £17,000 a year. Registrars can expect to earn around £25,000 a year. Superintendent registrars may earn up to £40,000 a year. Part-time celebrants usually earn a set fee for each ceremony they conduct.

Entry requirements

To become a registrar, you will need experience of dealing with a wide range of people, and you should be computer literate. You may find it useful to have some experience of public speaking. A driving licence is also useful.

Employers look for a good standard of general education and will usually prefer you to be qualified to at least GCSE standard or equivalent, including English and maths. In Scotland applicants need three S-Grades (1-3) including English. Doctors, midwives, ministers of religion, funeral directors and anyone working in the life assurance industry are not allowed to become registrars.

More information

LG careers
www.lgcareers.com

****

7. CONSTRUCTION

Although the construction industry is contracting at this point in time, there are always many opportunities within this area for a variety of different skills. One truism about this industry is that it expands and contracts regularly and the government is always using construction to try to get the economy going.

The following jobs are outlined below:

- Architect
- Bricklayer
- Building surveyor
- Building control officer
- Carpenters/joiners
- Civil engineer
- Clerk of works
- Electrician
- Gas service engineer
- Painter/decorator
- Plasterer
- Plumber
- Quantity surveyor
- Town planner

For more information on all jobs in the construction industry go to:

Construction Skills
Bircham Newton
King's Lynn
Norfolk
PE31 6RH
Tel: 0344 994 4400
www.cskills.org

ARCHITECT

The nature of the work

Architects draw plans for new buildings, and for restoring and conserving old ones. Their work also involves planning the layout of groups of buildings and the spaces around them.

To be an architect you will have to finish a five-year university course and complete at least two years' professional experience.

You would be responsible for a building project from the earliest stage through to completion. On larger jobs, you could work in a team alongside other architects and architectural technicians or technologists.

What can you earn?

As an architect's assistant during the trainee stages, you could earn between £17,000 and £30,000 a year.

Newly registered architects may earn between £30,000 and £35,000. With three to five years' post-registration experience, you may earn between around £34,000 and £42,000.

Entry requirements

The most common way to qualify as an architect involves:

- five years' study on a university course recognised for registration with the Architects Registration Board (ARB) **and** at least two years' professional experience.

See the RIBA and ARB websites for full details of qualifications and alternative routes to becoming an architect.

More information

Royal Institution of British Architects (RIBA)
66 Portland Place
London
W1B 1AD
Tel: 020 7580 5533
www.architecture.com

Architects Registration Board
Tel: 020 7580 5861
www.arb.org.uk

BRICKLAYER

The nature of the work

Bricklayers build and repair walls, chimney stacks, tunnel linings and decorative stonework like archways. They might also refurbish brickwork and masonry on restoration projects. As a bricklayer the projects you might work on can range from a house extension to a large commercial development. If you enjoy doing practical things and you are interested in construction, this could be the perfect job for you.

What can you earn?

A bricklaying labourer can earn up to £15,000 a year. Qualified bricklayers can earn between £16,000 and £23,000 a year. Experienced bricklayers, including instructors, can earn up to £30,000 a year. Overtime and various allowances can add to your income. Self-employed bricklayers set their own pay rates.

Entry requirements

You do not need formal qualifications to become a bricklayer, but employers usually want people who have some on-site experience. If you have not worked in construction before, you could find a job as a labourer to get site experience. Once you are working, your employer may be willing to offer you training in bricklaying.

You may be able to get into this job through an Apprenticeship scheme with a building company. Some building companies may want you to have GCSEs in subjects like maths, English, and design and technology, or vocational qualifications such as the BTEC Introductory Certificate or Diploma in Construction. You will need to check which schemes are available in your area and what the requirements are. To find out more, visit the Apprenticeships website.

Another option is to take a college course in bricklaying. This would teach you some of the skills needed for the job, but employers may still want you to have some site experience.

Courses include:

- BTEC Level 2 Certificate/Diploma in Construction (bricklaying options)
- City & Guilds Certificate in Basic Construction Skills: Bricklaying
- CSkills Intermediate/Advanced Construction Award (Trowel Occupations – Bricklaying).

For more information about bricklaying qualifications, see the ConstructionSkills website and contact your local college. ConstructionSkills also has general information on careers and qualifications in building. www.cskills.org

Traditional Building Skills Bursary Scheme

The aim of the Traditional Building Skills Bursary scheme is to reduce the shortage of skills in the traditional crafts and built heritage sector. It is doing this by offering bursaries and organising work-based training placements for suitable applicants.

To find out more about the scheme, suitability and available placements, visit the Traditional Building Skills Bursary Scheme website.

BUILDING SURVEYOR

The nature of the work
As a surveyor, you would usually focus on three main areas – surveying, legal work, and planning and inspection. Your work could include:

- surveying properties, identifying structural faults and making recommendations for repairs
- assessing damage for insurance purposes, for example following a fire or flooding
- establishing who is responsible for building repair costs

69

- advising clients on issues such as property boundary disputes
- acting as a client's supporter or standing as an expert witness during legal proceedings
- checking properties to make sure that they meet building regulations, and fire safety and accessibility standards
- dealing with planning applications and with improvement or conservation grants.

Depending on the size of the company, you may cover all of these tasks or you might specialise in just one.

Other duties would include supervising a surveying team made up of assistants and technicians.

What can you earn?

Newly-qualified graduates earn between £18,000 and £22,000 a year.

Experienced surveyors earn between £23,000 and £38,000 a year, and senior staff with chartered status can earn over £50,000 a year.

Entry requirements

To qualify as a building surveyor, you will need to complete a degree course accredited by the Royal Institution of Chartered Surveyors (RICS), followed by professional development. surveying

To search for accredited qualifications, see the RICS Courses website.

You could also start work in a trainee position with a surveying firm, and study for qualifications while you are working.

If you have a non-accredited degree, you will need to take a postgraduate course in surveying. You can do this through a company graduate traineeship, or by studying full-time at a RICS-accredited university. If you are working in engineering or construction, you could take a distance learning postgraduate conversion course with the College of Estate Management (CEM). For more details, see the CEM website.

With an HNC/HND or a foundation degree in surveying or construction, you may be able to start working as a surveying technician and take further qualifications to become a building surveyor.

For more information about surveying careers, accredited degree programmes and membership routes, contact the RICS and the Chartered Institute of Building's (CIOB) Faculty for Architecture and Surveying.

More information

Royal Institution of Chartered Surveyors (RICS)
Parliament Square
London
SW1P 3AD
Tel: 020 7334 3875
www.rics.org

College of Estate Management
Whiteknights
Reading
Berkshire
RG6 6AW
Tel: 0800 019 9697
www.cem.ac.uk

BUILDING CONTROL OFFICER

The nature of the work

As a building control officer, you would work on the planning and construction phases of building projects. These could range from a small housing extension to a large city centre redevelopment.

You would also be responsible for surveying buildings that have been damaged by fire or bad weather. If necessary, you could approve their demolition. Other responsibilities may include authorising entertainment licences, and checking safety at sports grounds, open-air events, cinemas and theatres.

On all projects you would have to take into account the implications of your decisions on contractors' time and costs. If you decided that a building project no longer meets regulations, you could start legal proceedings to change or stop the work.

What can you earn?

Starting salaries can range from £21,000 to £26,000 a year.

Experienced inspectors can earn between £27,000 and £38,000, and senior inspectors can earn up to £50,000 a year.

Rates tend to be higher in the South East, particularly in the private sector.

Entry requirements

You would normally need at least two A levels, a BTEC National Diploma, HNC/HND or a degree to work as a building control officer. Relevant subjects include:

- building studies
- civil engineering
- building control
- building surveying.

Employers' entry requirements can vary so you would need to check with them for exact details.

More information

www.lgcareers.com
Parliament Square
London
SW1P 3AD
Tel: 020 7334 3875
www.rics.org

Association of Building Engineers
Lutyens House
Billing Brook Road
Weston Favell
Northampton
NN3 8NW
Tel: 0845 126 1058
www.abe.org.uk

Chartered Institute of Building
Englemere
Kings Ride
Ascot
Berkshire
SL5 7TB
Tel: 01344 630700
www.ciob.org.uk

CARPENTER OR JOINER

The nature of the work
As a carpenter or joiner, you may work in one or more of the following areas:

- cutting and shaping timber for floorboards, skirting boards and window frames
- making and assembling doors, window frames, staircases and fitted furniture
- fitting wooden structures, like floor and roof joists, roof timbers, staircases, partition walls, and door and window frames (first fixings)
- installing skirting boards, door surrounds, doors, cupboards and shelving, as well as door handles and locks (second fixings)
- building temporary wooden supports for concrete that is setting, for example on motorway bridge supports or building foundations (formwork)
- making and fitting interiors for shops, hotels, banks, offices and public buildings.

You could be skilled in all of these or you may specialise in just one or two.

What can you earn?
Starting salaries are between £13,000 and £16,000 a year.

Qualified joiners earn between £17,000 and £23,000 a year, and experienced joiners can earn up to £28,000 a year.

Overtime and shift allowances will increase your income. Self-employed carpenters and joiners set their own rates.

Entry requirements

You do not need any formal qualifications to become a carpenter or joiner, but employers usually want people with some on-site experience. If you have not worked in construction before, you could work as a joiner's mate or labourer to get site experience. Once working, your employer may offer you training in carpentry and joinery.

You may be able to become a carpenter or joiner through an Apprenticeship scheme. To be eligible, you may need GCSEs in subjects such as maths, English and design and technology, or vocational qualifications such as a BTEC Certificate or Diploma in Construction (carpentry options). To find out more about Apprenticeships, visit the Apprenticeships website.

Another route in is to take a college course in carpentry and joinery. This would give you some of the skills needed for the job, but employers may still want to see some site experience.

Courses include:

- City & Guilds Award in Basic Construction Skills (carpentry options)
- CSkills Level 2 Diploma in Site Carpentry.

For more details about courses, contact ConstructionSkills and your local college. ConstructionSkills also has general information on building careers and qualifications.

Traditional Building Skills Bursary Scheme

The Traditional Building Skills Bursary scheme aims to increase the number of skilled people in the traditional crafts and built heritage sector. It is doing this by offering grants (bursaries) and organising work-based training placements for suitable applicants. To find out more, visit the Traditional Building Skills Bursary Scheme website.

More information

National Heritage Training Group
www.nhtg.org.uk

Institute of Carpenters (IOC)
32 High Street
Wendover
Buckinghamshire
HP22 6EA
www.instituteofcarpenters.com

Construction Skills Certification Scheme (CSCS)
Tel: 0844 576 8777
www.cscs.uk.com

Construction Skills
Bircham Newton
King's Lynn
Norfolk
PE31 6RH
Tel: 0344 994 4400
www.cskills.org

CIVIL ENGINEER

The nature of the work

You could work in any one of the following specialist areas of engineering:

- structural – dams, buildings, offshore platforms and pipelines
- transportation – roads, railways, canals and airports
- environmental – water supply networks, drainage and flood barriers
- maritime – ports, harbours and sea defences
- geotechnical – mining, earthworks and construction foundations.

What can you earn?

Graduate salaries are between £17,000 and £25,000 a year. Experienced engineers earn between £25,000 and £40,000 a year, and senior Chartered Engineers can earn between £60,000 and £100,000 a year.

Entry requirements

You would normally need to gain a three-year Bachelor of Engineering (BEng) degree or four-year Masters (MEng) degree in civil engineering for this career. These qualifications are important if you want to work towards incorporated or chartered engineer status. See the Training and Development section below for details. You could study other engineering-related subjects, but it may take you longer to fully qualify.

To do a degree course, you will need at least five GCSEs (A-C) and two or three A levels, including maths and a science subject (normally physics), or equivalent qualifications. Check exact entry requirements with individual colleges and universities, as they may accept a relevant Access to Higher Education award.

If you already work in the industry as a technician, you could qualify as a civil engineer by studying part-time for a BTEC HNC/HND, foundation degree or degree in civil engineering.

More information about engineering careers and courses is on the Institution of Civil Engineers (ICE) website.

More information

Institution of Structural Engineers (ISE)
11 Upper Belgrave Street
London
SW1X 8BH
Tel: 020 7235 4535
www.istructe.org.uk

The UKRC
Listerhills Park of Science and Commerce
40-42 Campus Road
Bradford
BD7 1HR
Tel: 01274 436485
www.theukrc.org

Institution of Civil Engineers
Great George Street
London
SW1P 3AA
Tel: 020 7222 7722
www.ice.org.uk

Construction Skills
Bircham Newton
King's Lynn
Norfolk
PE31 6RH
Tel: 0344 994 4400
www.cskills.org

Tomorrows Engineers
EngineeringUK
Weston House
246 High Holborn
London
WC1V 7EX
Email: careers@engineeringuk.com
Tel: 020 3206 0400
www.tomorrowsengineers.org.uk

Engineering Training Council (NI)
Interpoint
20-24 York Street
Belfast
BT15 1AQ
Tel: 028 9032 9878
www.etcni.org.uk

CLERK OF WORKS

The nature of the work
As a clerk of works, or site inspector, you would oversee the quality and safety of work on a construction site, making sure that building plans and specifications are being followed correctly.

Your duties would include:

- performing regular inspections of the work on site and comparing completed work with drawings and specifications
- measuring and sampling building materials to check their quality

- recording results either on paper or a hand-held Personal Digital Assistant (PDA)
- identifying defects and suggesting ways to correct them
- liaising with other construction staff, such as contractors, engineers and surveyors
- monitoring and reporting progress to construction managers, architects and clients

You may also be responsible for supervising the workforce on the building site during a project.

What can you earn?

A clerk of works can earn between £21,000 and £40,000 year. With substantial experience, this can rise to around £50,000 or higher, depending on the contract.

Entry requirements

You would usually become a clerk of works after gaining experience in the construction or engineering industries, at craft or technician level.

You could look for work as a trainee after taking a BTEC HNC/HND, foundation degree or degree in construction or engineering, and work your way up. To search for colleges and universities offering these courses, visit the UCAS website.

Employers may insist that you hold membership of the Institute of Clerks of Works and Construction Inspectorate (ICWCI), which is the recognised industry body for this area of work. See the further training section below for more details.

To find out more about this career, visit the CITB-ConstructionSkills websites.

More information

Institute of Clerks of Works and Construction Inspectors
28 Commerce Rd
Lynch Wood
Peterborough
PE2 6LR

Tel: 01733 405160
www.icwgb.org

Construction Skills CITB
Bircham Newton
King's Lynn
Norfolk
PE31 6RH
Tel: 0344 994 4400
www.cskills.org

Construction Skills Certification Sceme
Tel: 0844 576 8777
www.cscs.uk.com

ELECTRICIAN

The nature of the work
If you are interested in electrics and like the idea of diverse and exciting work, this could be a great career for you.

Electricians work on a very wide range of projects, from bringing power to homes to taking part in major engineering projects. Their tasks can range from transporting data along fibre optic cables to programming computer-controlled 'intelligent' buildings and factories. They can also work with renewable technology, such as wind turbines or photovoltaic systems that turn the sun's energy into electricity.

As an electrician, you would install, inspect and test equipment, ensure that electrotechnical systems work, and spot and fix faults.

Electrotechnical careers are divided into different areas:

Installation electrician - Installing power systems, lighting, fire protection, security and data-network systems in all different types of buildings.

- Maintenance electrician - Checking systems regularly to ensure that they keep on working efficiently and safely.
- Electrotechnical panel builders - Having responsibility for the building and installing control panels that operate the electrical systems inside buildings.

- Machine repair and rewind electrician - Repairing and maintaining electrical motors and other machinery such as transformers to make sure that they work correctly.
- Highway systems electrician - Installing and maintaining street lighting and traffic management systems that tell the public what they need to know when they're on the roads and motorways.

You could be working in all types of buildings, such as homes, offices, shops or sports stadiums. You may also supervise other people in a team.

Depending on your exact role, you may work on a construction site, which can be noisy, dusty and cold. You might have to work in cramped and uncomfortable spaces to reach the electrical cabling and equipment, and you may sometimes work at heights using a variety of equipment such as scaffolding.

What can you earn?

First year apprentices may start on around £8,000 a year.

Newly-qualified electricians may earn over £17,000 a year, and experienced electricians may earn over £30,000 a year.

Some employers pay more, and you might get bonuses and overtime pay. Your salary will vary depending on your employer and where you live in the UK.

There are national set rates to cover travelling time, travel expenses and accommodation costs.

Entry requirements

To work as a qualified electrician, you will need to gain an NVQ Diploma or Scottish Vocational Qualification (SVQ) at Level 3. You may also need additional training if you want to do specialist work such as installing environmental technology systems.

You could start as an apprentice straight from school or college. You would combine training on the job with going to a college or training centre. It normally takes between three and a half and four years to complete training and an apprenticeship.

If you're not able to do an apprenticeship straight away, there are programmes around the UK that can help you to progress to an apprenticeship, further learning or a job. Speak to your local careers adviser to find out more.

Some apprenticeship schemes are open to people over 25, although the number of places might be limited. If you are over 25 and employed, or you could be assessed on site, you could work towards the NVQ Diploma/SVQ without doing an apprenticeship.

The range of Apprenticeships available in your area will depend on the local jobs market and the types of skills employers need from their workers. To find out more, visit the Apprenticeships website.

Electricians qualified before 1996

If you qualified as an electrician before 1996, you should contact the Joint Industry Board for the Electrical Contracting Industry (JIB). They will assess your experience and qualifications to decide whether you meet their requirements. They will be able to tell you if you need to take further qualifications.

Overseas qualified electricians

If you have qualified as an electrician outside the UK, you could register with the JIB Electrotechnical Card Scheme (ECS). You will need to do three things to register:

- contact UK NARIC to find out what your qualifications match in the UK
- complete the City & Guilds 17th Edition IEE Wiring Regulations (2382)
- pass the ECS Health and Safety Assessment.

You may also need to contact the certification schemes listed below for details of how to meet Part P requirements of the Building Regulations (see Training and Development section below for more about Part P).

You may need a driving licence.

Portable Appliance Testing (PAT)

If your job involves carrying out portable appliance testing (also known as PAT testing), you will need to have relevant training. The City & Guilds In-service Inspection and Testing of Electrical Equipment (2377) course is a common choice. Any course that meets the IEE Codes of Practice would be suitable.

You do not always have to be a qualified electrician to carry out PAT testing, however, you would need to show your capability. This is normally shown by qualifications and/or relevant experience. For more details, visit the PAT Testing Information website.

Electrical Safety and Part P

Part P of the Building Regulations states that certain types of household electrical work must be approved by a certified contractor or building inspector. You can certify your own work by completing a short Part P training scheme. See the Part P contacts in More Information below for details about certification training, entry requirements and information about the electrical work that requires approval.

Entry requirements for a training scheme will depend on your qualifications and experience. Some providers offer extra training if you need it, for instance, 17th Edition Wiring Regulations. Some do not, so please check with the providers.

Traditional Building Skills Bursary Scheme

The aim of the Traditional Building Skills Bursary scheme is to reduce the shortage of skills in the traditional crafts and built heritage sector. It is doing this by offering bursaries and organising work-based training placements for suitable applicants.

To find out more about the scheme, suitability and available placements, visit the Traditional Building Skills Bursary Scheme website.

Environmental Technologies

The government has set targets for greater energy efficiency. With further training, you may be able to install and maintain renewable energy technologies like solar electric systems. Some employers may also pay half the cost of training for qualifications in environmental technologies like fitting solar heating systems.

To find out more about this growing area of work, see the following websites:

You could continue your professional development by gaining higher qualifications such as NVQ Diploma/SVQ Level 4, a foundation degree, HNC, HND or degree in Building Services Engineering. If you want to do a degree course, many universities or similar institutions will accept a relevant qualification, or take your work experience into account, instead of traditional academic qualifications.

You can search for full-time courses on the Universities and Colleges Admissions Service (UCAS) website, or contact individual universities or colleges for information about part-time courses.

The Institution of Engineering and Technology (IET) offers a membership scheme at various grades. Membership would give you access to a variety of professional development workshops and training courses. See the IET website for more information.

More information

Summit Skills
Tel: 08000 688336
www.summitskills.org.uk

Electrical Contractors Association
www.eca.co.uk

Part P Self-Certification Schemes:

NICEIC Domestic Installer Scheme
Tel: 0870 013 0382
www.niceic.org.uk

ELECSA
Tel: 0870 749 0080
www.elecsa.org.uk

British Standards Institution
Tel: 01442 278607
www.bsi-global.com

National Association for Professional Testers and Inspectors
Tel: 0870 444 1392
www.napit.org.uk

GAS SERVICE TECHNICIAN

The nature of the work

As a gas service technician, you would mainly work at customers' homes, or at businesses like cafes and hotel kitchens. Your job could include:

- installing appliances and systems
- carrying out planned maintenance checks on systems and equipment
- testing controls and safety devices to make sure that they are working properly
- finding and repairing gas leaks using computerised fault-finding equipment
- replacing or repairing faulty or old parts
- ordering new parts when necessary
- keeping records of work you have carried out
- giving customers advice about gas safety and energy efficiency.

You would also give customers quotes for jobs and tell them how long they would take, sell additional company services and occasionally deal with complaints. Gas service technicians are also sometimes known as gas installation engineers or gas maintenance engineers.

What can you earn?

British Gas apprenticeship salaries are around £15,000 a year. Qualified technicians can earn between £19,000 and £30,000 a year.

Bonuses, shift allowances and overtime will increase basic salaries.

Entry requirements

To qualify as a gas service technician you will need:

- NVQ Level 3 in Domestic Natural Gas Installation (you normally need to be employed by a company to complete this); or
- appropriate work experience and training leading to safety certification through the Accredited Certification Scheme (ACS).

You will also need to have Gas Safe Registration (this used to be called CORGI registration).

See the Training and Development section below for more details.

You may be able to start this career through an Apprenticeship scheme. You will need to check which schemes are available in your area. To find out more, visit the Apprenticeships website.

Some utility companies offer national apprenticeship schemes in a variety of technical and engineering roles. For more information, see the Energy and Utility Skills website.

Industry organisations strongly recommend that you gain a work placement or job with a gas servicing firm as soon as possible after starting the Technical Certificate (the theory part of the NVQ). This would allow you to work towards the full NVQ. Your college may help you to find a placement, but you could also contact companies directly.

You may need a driving licence, as this job normally involves travelling to customer's premises.

Accredited Certification Scheme (ACS)

If you have experience in the gas industry or related fields, you may be able to follow the ACS scheme. This would enable you to demonstrate your ability to work safely with gas systems and equipment, and be eligible to join the Gas Safe Register. You will need to complete safety assessments covering your specific areas of work and the types of appliances you work on every five years.

If you have qualifications from any other fields, you will have to be trained and satisfy safety assessments at an approved ACS centre.

You will be classed as being in one of three categories when you apply for ACS assessment:

Oil-fired equipment

If you work with oil-fired equipment, such as heating systems and oil storage tanks, you could gain accreditation with the Oil Firing Technical Association for the Petroleum Industry (OFTEC). Contact OFTEC for more information.

Energy efficiency

You could also gain the City & Guilds Certificate in Energy Efficiency for Domestic Heating, which will give you the knowledge and competence you need to meet Part L of the Building Regulations concerning energy efficiency.

More information

Gas safe Register
Tel: 0800 408 5500
www.gassaferegister.co.uk

Oil Firing Technical Association for the Petroleum Industry
Foxwood House
Dobbs Lane
Kesgrave
Ipswich
IP5 2QQ
Tel: 0845 658 5080
www.oftec.co.uk

British Gas Jobs
The Harrow Way
Basingstoke
Hampshire
RG22 4AR
www.britishgasjobs.co.uk

Energy and Utility Skills
Friars Gate

1011 Stratford Road
Shirley
Solihull
B90 4BN
Tel: 0845 077 9922
www.euskills.co.uk

Tomorrows Engineers
EngineeringUK
Weston House
246 High Holborn
London
WC1V 7EX
Email: careers@engineeringuk.com
Tel: 020 3206 0400
www.tomorrowsengineers.org.uk

PAINTER AND DECORATOR

The nature of the work

As a painter and decorator, you would work on a variety of domestic and industrial projects ranging from re-decorating homes to applying heavy-duty finishes to large structures like bridges.

On a domestic job, you would use paint, varnishes and wallpaper to decorate rooms. You would follow the householder's instructions about choice of colour, finishing texture and wallpaper patterns. Your main tasks would include:

measuring surface areas to work out how much paint or wall covering you need

- stripping off old wallpaper or paint
- filling holes and cracks and making sure surfaces are level
- preparing surfaces with primer and undercoat
- mixing paint to the right shade, either by hand or using computerised colour-matching equipment
- applying layers of paint and hanging wallpaper
- tidying up after finishing a job.

On some jobs you might apply specialist finishes such as rag rolling, graining and marbling. You would often work from ladders or raised platforms to reach ceilings.

For industrial projects, such as bridges or ships, you would remove old paintwork with abrasive blasting methods before applying new coatings using industrial paint spraying equipment. You would use a cradle or safety harness when working.

Paints and solvents give off fumes, so you may have to wear a protective mask or use fume extraction equipment on some jobs, if in enclosed spaces.

What can you earn?

Starting salaries can be between £13,500 and £16,500 a year.

Average salaries for qualified painters and decorators are between £17,000 and £21,500 a year. Decorators with supervisor duties or specialist skills can earn over £23,000 a year.

Overtime and shift allowances can increase income. Self-employed painters and decorators set their own pay rates.

Entry requirements

Employers often prefer people with some relevant experience, so you could start by looking for work as a painter and decorator's labourer or 'mate'. Once you are working, your employer may give you the opportunity for further training in painting and decorating. See the Training and Development section below for more details.

Another option is to take a college course, which would give you some of the skills needed for the job. Relevant courses include:

- City & Guilds Level 1 Certificate in Basic Construction Skills (Painting and Decorating)
- CSkills Level 1 Diploma in Painting and Decorating
- CSkills Intermediate and Advanced Construction Award (Decorative Occupations – Painting and Decorating).

For more details about courses and entry requirements, contact your local colleges.

A common way into this career is through an Apprenticeship scheme. You will need to check which schemes are available in your area. To do an Apprenticeship, you may need GCSEs in subjects such as maths, English and design and technology, or equivalent qualifications such as the BTEC Introductory Certificate and Diploma in Construction. This course includes options in painting and decorating.

To find out more about Apprenticeships, see the Apprenticeships website.

For more information about careers and qualifications in painting and decorating, see the bConstructive website.

The Know Your Place campaign promotes the construction trades as a career choice for women. See the Know Your Place website for details.

Traditional Building Skills Bursary Scheme

The aim of the Traditional Building Skills Bursary scheme is to reduce the shortage of skills in the traditional crafts and built heritage sector. It is doing this by offering bursaries and organising work-based training placements for suitable applicants.

To find out more about the scheme, suitability and available placements, see the Traditional Building Skills Bursary Scheme website.

More information

Industrial Rope Trade association
Kingsley House
Ganders Business Park
Kingsley
Bordon
Hampshire
GU35 9LU
Tel: 01420 471619
www.irata.org

National Heritage Training Group
www.nhtg.org.uk

Construction Skills Certification Scheme (CSCS)
Tel: 0844 576 8777
www.cscs.uk.com

ConstructionSkills
Bircham Newton
King's Lynn
Norfolk
PE31 6RH
Tel: 0344 994 4400
www.cskills.org

PLASTERER

The nature of the work

You would normally be part of a small team, and work in one of the following:

- solid plastering – applying wet finishes to surfaces and putting protective coverings like pebble-dashing on external walls
- fibrous plastering – creating ornamental plasterwork, such as ceiling roses, cornices, and architraves, using a mixture of plaster and short fibres shaped with moulds and casts
- dry lining – fixing internal plasterboard or wallboard partitions by fastening them together on a timber or metal frame ready for decorating.

You could work on small-scale domestic jobs, repairs and restoration or on big commercial developments such as schools or hospitals.

What can you earn?

Starting salaries can be between £14,000 and £17,000 a year. Qualified plasterers can earn from £17,500 to over £25,000 or more. Experienced plasterers can earn around £28,000 a year.

Overtime and shift allowances will increase earnings. Self-employed plasterers negotiate their own rates.

Entry requirements

You do not usually need qualifications to become a plasterer, but employers usually look for people with some on-site experience. If you have not worked in construction before, you may be able to get this experience by working as a plasterer's 'mate' or labourer.

A common way into plastering is through an Apprenticeship scheme with a plastering, drylining or building firm. The range of Apprenticeships available in your area will depend on the local jobs market and the types of skills employers need from their workers. For more information, visit the Apprenticeships website.

For an Apprenticeship, you may need some GCSEs in subjects such as maths, English and design and technology, or equivalent qualifications.

Alternatively, you could learn some of the skills needed for the job by taking a college course in plastering, but employers may still want to see some site experience. Relevant courses include:

- City & Guilds (6217) Certificate in Basic Construction Skills (Plastering)
- CSkills Awards Diploma in Plastering
- ABC Certificate in Preparation for Employment in Plastering
- Ascentis Preparation for Employment in the Construction Industries (Plastering).

Visit the ConstructionSkills website for information on construction careers and qualifications.

The Know Your Place campaign aims to promote the construction industry as a career choice for women.

More information

National Heritage Training Group
www.nhtg.org.uk

Construction Skills Certification Scheme (CSCS)
Tel: 0844 576 8777
www.cscs.uk.com

Construction Skills CITB
Bircham Newton
King's Lynn
Norfolk
PE31 6RH
Tel: 0344 994 4400
www.cskills.org

PLUMBER

The nature of the work

Depending on whether you work in homes, industrial or commercial locations, your job could include:

- installing and repairing water supplies, heating systems and drainage
- servicing gas and oil-fired central heating systems, boilers and radiators
- installing and fixing domestic appliances like showers and washing machines
- servicing air-conditioning and ventilation units
- fitting weather-proof materials, joints and flashings to roofs, chimneys and walls.

On all jobs you would use hand and power tools, which could include welding equipment.

As an experienced plumber, you might specialise in sheet metal work for industrial, commercial or historical buildings.

What can you earn?

Starting salaries for newly qualified plumbers can be between £16,500 and £21,000 a year. Experienced plumbers can earn between £21,000 and £35,000 a year.

Rates vary in different regions. The highest average salaries are in London and the South East.

Self-employed plumbers set their own rates.

Entry requirements

To become a qualified plumber you will need to achieve Level 2 and 3 NVQ Diplomas from City & Guilds or EAL. These are:

- City & Guilds (6189) NVQ Diploma in Plumbing and Domestic Heating, at levels 2 and 3
- EAL NVQ Diploma in Domestic Heating and Plumbing at levels 2 and 3.

If you are not working in plumbing at the moment, you would start at level 2. At this level you would first need to gain passes in a series of knowledge units. You would then move on to practical units, which you would mainly complete in the workplace.

Note: These qualifications replace the City & Guilds (6129) Technical Certificate and the NVQ levels 2 and 3 in Mechanical Engineering Services – Plumbing (City & Guilds 6089). If you are already part way through these qualifications, you will be able to finish them and they will still be valid for you to work as plumber.

There is strong competition for places on plumbing courses, and college entry requirements will often include an aptitude test. Due to health and safety regulations, you may not be able to do a training course if you are colour blind. Check with your chosen college and ask if they can offer you a colour vision assessment test.

Industry organisations strongly recommend that you get a work placement or employment with a plumbing firm soon after starting your training. This would allow you to complete the practical units of the NVQ Diplomas. Your college may help you find a placement but you could also contact plumbing firms directly.

The Chartered Institute of Plumbing and Heating Engineering (CIPHE) has useful information for anyone wanting to train as a plumber. Visit the CIPHE website for more details.

See the SummitSkills website for further information on entry routes into plumbing, training providers and new qualifications.

Entry into plumbing in Northern Ireland is similar to training in England and Wales. For more details contact ConstructionSkills (NI) and SNIPEF.

Apprenticeships

You may be able to become a qualified plumber through an Apprenticeship scheme. To get on to a scheme you will normally need four GCSEs (grades A-C). You will need to check if there are schemes running in your areas. To find out more, visit the Apprenticeships website.

Short courses

A number of organisations offer short intensive training courses, some with home study options. You should check whether the course you choose is recognised and accredited by the industry. Your regional City & Guilds office will be able to check this for you. You should also ask the course provider what would happen if you fell behind or dropped out of an intensive course.

Overseas qualifications

If you qualified outside the UK, contact the Joint Industry Board for Plumbing for information about how to register as a qualified plumber. You will need to tell them which qualifications you have from your home country.

More information

SummitSkills
Tel: 08000 688336
www.summitskills.org.uk

CITB ConstructionSkills (NI)
17 Dundrod Road
Nutts Corner
Crumlin
Co Antrim
BT29 4SR
Tel: 0800 587 2288
http://www.citbni.org.uk

Scottish and Northern Ireland Plumbing Employers Federation (SNIPEF)
2 Walker Street
Edinburgh

EH3 7LB
Tel: 0131 225 2255 www.snipef.org

Joint Industry Board for Plumbing Mechanical Engineering Services
Tel: 01480 476925
www.jib-pmes.org.uk

British Plumbing Employers Council Services Ltd (BPEC Services Ltd)
2 Walker Street
Edinburgh
EH3 7LB
www.bpec.org.uk/services

Institute of Plumbing and Heating Engineers
(including Women in Plumbing Group)
64 Station Lane
Hornchurch
Essex
RM12 6NB
Tel: 01708 472791
www.iphe.org.uk

Gas Safe Register
Tel: 0800 408 5500
www.gassaferegister.co.uk

QUANTITY SURVEYOR

The nature of the work
As a quantity surveyor, you might work on:

- housing and industrial sites
- retail and commercial developments
- roads, rail and waterways.

On most projects, your main responsibilities would be:

- carrying out feasibility studies to estimate materials, time and labour costs
- negotiating and drawing up bids for tenders and contracts

- monitoring each stage of construction to make sure that costs are in line with forecasts
- providing financial progress reports to clients
- advising clients on legal and contractual matters
- acting on clients' behalf to resolve disputes
- assessing the financial costs of new environmental guidelines, such as using sustainable timber.

You would use computer software to carry out some of these tasks, and to keep records, prepare work schedules and write reports. You might also deal with the maintenance and renovation costs once buildings are in use.

What can you earn?

Starting salaries can be between £20,000 and £25,000 a year. With experience this can rise to between £25,000 and £45,000. Senior chartered quantity surveyors can earn between £50,000 and £80,000 a year.

Entry requirements

You need a degree or professional qualification accredited by the Royal Institution for Chartered Surveyors (RICS) to qualify as a chartered quantity surveyor. Relevant subjects include:

- surveying
- construction
- civil engineering
- structural engineering.

If you are already working in engineering or construction, you could take a part-time distance learning postgraduate degree while working – many of RICS's accredited postgraduate degrees are available part-time or distance learning.

If you have a BTEC HNC, HND or foundation degree in surveying, you may be able to start work as a surveying technician then complete further study to qualify as a quantity surveyor.

You can find out more about careers and courses in surveying, by visiting the Royal Institution of Chartered Surveyors (RICS) and Chartered Institute of Building (CIOB) websites.

More information

Royal Institution of Chartered Surveyors (RICS)
Parliament Square
London
SW1P 3AD
Tel: 0207 334 3875
www.rics.org

College of Estate Management
Whiteknights
Reading
Berkshire
RG6 6AW
Tel: 0800 019 9697
www.cem.ac.uk

Chartered Institute of Building
Englemere
Kings Ride
Ascot
Berkshire
SL5 7TB
Tel: 01344 630700
www.ciob.org.uk

Construction Industry Council (CIC)
26 Store Street
London
WC1E 7BT
Tel: 0207 399 7400
www.cicskills.org.uk

ROOFER

The nature of the work

If you have a head for heights and are able to understand building plans, this job could suit you. As a roofer, your work could range from re-slating the roof on a house, to restoring the lead sheets on an old building.

97

In this job you will need good number skills to work out quantities of goods and prices. You will also need to work flexibly as part of a team.

It is common to start out as a roofing labourer and then get training on the job. Alternatively, you could do a course in roof slating and tiling first, which would teach you some of the skills you would need. You may be able to get into this job through an Apprenticeship.

What can you earn?

A roofing labourer or trainee can earn from £13,000 to £15,000 a year. Once qualified this can rise to between £16,000 and £24,000. Experienced roofers can earn up to £31,000 a year. Overtime and shift allowances will increase wages, while self-employed roofers set their own rates.

Entry requirements

Finding work as an entry-level roofing labourer is a common way into this career, as it will give you the on-site experience employers often ask for. Once you are working, your employer may be willing to give you further training in roofing techniques.

You may be able to get into this career by completing an Apprenticeship with a building or roofing company. The range of Apprenticeships available in your area will depend on the local jobs market and the types of skills employers need from their workers. To find out more, visit the Apprenticeships website.

To get on to an Apprenticeship, you may need GCSEs (grades A-C) in subjects like maths, English and design and technology. Equivalent qualifications like the BTEC Certificate or Diploma in Construction may also be accepted.

Alternatively, you could take a college course, such as the ConstructionSkills Awards Level 2 Diploma in Roof Slating and Tiling, which would teach you some of the skills needed. However, employers may still ask for some site experience. Check with local colleges for course availability and entry requirements.

See the ConstructionSkills website for more information on construction careers and qualifications.

The Know Your Place campaign aims to promote the construction trades as a career choice for women. Visit the website for more details.

Traditional Building Skills Bursary Scheme

The Traditional Building Skills Bursary Scheme aims to address skills shortages within the traditional crafts and built heritage sector by offering bursaries and organising work-based training placements for eligible applicants.

To find out more about the scheme, eligibility and which placements are available, visit the Traditional Building Skills Bursary Scheme website.

More information

National Heritage Training Group
www.nhtg.org.uk

Institute of Roofing
Tel: 020 7448 3858
www.instituteofroofing.org

Construction Skills Certification Scheme (CSCS)
Tel: 0844 576 8777
www.cscs.uk.com

Construction Skills CITB
Bircham Newton
King's Lynn
Norfolk
PE31 6RH
Tel: 0344 994 4400
www.cskills.org

TOWN PLANNER

The nature of the work
As a town planner (or spatial planner) you would help to shape the way towns and cities develop. This involves balancing the competing demands placed on land by housing, business, transport and leisure, and making sure plans meet

the economic and social needs of the community. If you are interested in urban environments, and you can see different viewpoints and make fair decisions, this job might suit you well.

To be good at this job you would also need to be a good communicator and negotiator. You would need knowledge of local planning policies and procedures. You would need report writing skills.

To work as a town planner you need a qualification accredited by the Royal Town Planning Institute (RTPI). You can qualify by studying for an RTPI-accredited degree in Town Planning. Alternatively, you can qualify by doing an RTPI-accredited postgraduate course, if you have a degree in a relevant subject such as surveying, architecture, statistics, geography or environmental science.

You would also assess the potential impact that developments, such as new road building, might have on an area. To do this, you would use surveying techniques, geographical information systems (GIS) and computer-aided design (CAD) to draw up plans and make recommendations to local and regional councils.

What can you earn?

For graduate or assistant planners this can be between £16,000 and £28,000 a year. Senior planners can earn up to £34,000. Planners with management responsibilities can earn up to £41,000. Chief planning officers can earn between £55,000 and £80,000.

Entry requirements

To work as a town planner you need a qualification accredited by the Royal Town Planning Institute (RTPI).

You can qualify by completing one of the following:

- a full-time RTPI-accredited degree course – these last for four years, which includes a three-year BA degree and a one-year postgraduate diploma (longer part-time courses are also available)
- an RTPI-accredited postgraduate course – If you already have a degree in a subject such as surveying, architecture, statistics, geography or environmental science

- a distance learning course at degree or postgraduate level – available jointly through the Open University and a consortium of the University of the West of England, Leeds Metropolitan University, London South Bank University and Dundee University.

Visit the RTPI website for a list of all accredited courses and information on town planning careers.

More information

Royal Town Planning Institute
41 Botolph Lane
London
EC3R 8DL
Tel: 020 7929 9494
www.rtpi.org.uk

LGcareers
www.lgcareers.com

Asset Skills
2 The Courtyard
48 New North Road
Exeter
Devon
EX4 4EP
Tel: 01392 423399
Careers Advice: careers@assetskills.org
www.assetskills.org

Local Government jobs
www.lgjobs.com

****

8. ENGINEERING

For those who want to join the long and illustrious line of great British engineers, this is the profession for you. However, there are many jobs within engineering and this chapter outlines the following:

- Civil engineer
- Mechanical engineer
- Design engineer
- Marine engineering technician

For more information on the many and diverse jobs in engineering, go to: www.tomorrowsengineers.org.uk

CIVIL ENGINEER

The nature of the work
You could work in any one of the following specialist areas of engineering:
- structural – dams, buildings, offshore platforms and pipelines
- transportation – roads, railways, canals and airports
- environmental – water supply networks, drainage and flood barriers
- maritime – ports, harbours and sea defences
- geotechnical – mining, earthworks and construction foundations.

You would normally work on projects alongside other professionals, such as architects, surveyors and building contractors. For more information about a career as a civil engineer see the Institution of Civil Engineers website.

What can you earn?

Graduate salaries are between £17,000 and £25,000 a year. Experienced engineers earn between £25,000 and £40,000 a year, and senior Chartered Engineers can earn between £60,000 and £100,000 a year.

Entry requirements

You would normally need to gain a three-year Bachelor of Engineering (BEng) degree or four-year Masters (MEng) degree in civil engineering for this career. These qualifications are important if you want to work towards incorporated or chartered engineer status. See the Training and Development section below for details. You could study other engineering-related subjects, but it may take you longer to fully qualify.

To do a degree course, you will need at least five GCSEs (A-C) and two or three A levels, including maths and a science subject (normally physics), or equivalent qualifications. Check exact entry requirements with individual colleges and universities, as they may accept a relevant Access to Higher Education award.

If you already work in the industry as a technician, you could qualify as a civil engineer by studying part-time for a BTEC HNC/HND, foundation degree or degree in civil engineering.

More information about engineering careers and courses is on the Institution of Civil Engineers (ICE) website.

For information on courses and careers in Northern Ireland, see the Engineering Training Council NI website.

More information

Institution of Structural Engineers
11 Upper Belgrave Street
London
SW1X 8BH
Tel: 020 7235 4535
www.istructe.org.uk

The UKRC
Listerhills Park of Science and Commerce
40-42 Campus Road
Bradford

BD7 1HR
Tel: 01274 436485
www.theukrc.org

Institution of Civil Engineers
Great George Street
London
SW1P 3AA
Tel: 020 7222 7722
www.ice.org.uk

Construction Skills
Bircham Newton
King's Lynn
Norfolk
PE31 6RH
Tel: 0344 994 4400
www.cskills.org

Tomorrow's Engineers
EngineeringUK
Weston House
246 High Holborn
London
WC1V 7EX
Email: careers@engineeringuk.com
Tel: 020 3206 0400
www.tomorrowsengineers.org.uk

Engineering Training Council (NI)
Interpoint
20-24 York Street
Belfast
BT15 1AQ
Tel: 028 9032 9878
www.etcni.org.uk

Construction Industry Council (CIC)
26 Store Street
London
WC1E 7BT
Tel: 020 7399 7400
www.cicskills.org.uk

___

MECHANICAL ENGINEER

The nature of the work

Your work would be divided into three key areas:

- research and development – assessing new products and innovations, and building prototypes
- design – turning research into technical plans using computer aided design/modelling (CAD/CAM) programs
- production – improving processes, and overseeing the installation of machinery and parts.

You could be working on large scale projects, for instance developing new ways to harness wave and tidal power; or at the small scale or micromechanical level, for example making prosthetic implants to help people become more mobile.

What can you earn?

Starting salaries can be between £19,500 and £22,000 a year. Experienced mechanical engineers can earn between £26,000 and £39,000. Engineers with chartered status can earn over £40,000 a year.

Entry requirements

To work as a mechanical engineer you will need a foundation degree, BTEC HNC/HND or degree in mechanical engineering, or a related engineering subject.

105

To search for foundation degrees, HNDs and degrees, see the Universities and Colleges Admissions Service (UCAS) website.

For a degree course you will usually need at least five GCSEs (grades A-C) and two or three A levels, possibly including maths and physics. Other science subjects such as biology would be useful for medical engineering. Check with colleges or universities for exact entry requirements, as alternative qualifications may be accepted.

Some courses, such as sandwich degrees, include a year in industry which may be useful when you start applying for work. Alternatively you could organise your own work placement with a relevant company.

You may also be able to get into this career starting off as an mechanical engineering technician apprentice with a manufacturer or engineering company and then after your Apprenticeship going on to higher education qualifications.

The range of Apprenticeships available in your area will depend on the local jobs market and the skills employers need from their workers. For more information, visit the Apprenticeships website.

To get on to an Apprenticeship, you are likely to need four or five GCSEs (A-C), including maths, English and a science subject.

For more information about careers in engineering, see the Institution of Mechanical Engineers and SEMTA websites.

More information

SEMTA (Sector Skills Council for Science, Engineering and Manufacturing Technologies in the UK)
14 Upton Road
Watford
Hertfordshire
WD18 0JT
Tel: 0845 643 9001
www.semta.org.uk

Women in Science Engineering and Construction
UK Resource Centre
Athlone Wing
Old Building
Great Horton Road
Bradford
BD7 1AY
Tel: 01274 436485
www.theukrc.org/wise

Institution of Mechanical Engineers
1 Birdcage Walk
Westminster
London
SW1H 9JJ
Tel: 020 7222 7899
www.imeche.org

Engineering Training Council (Northern Ireland)
Interpoint
20-24 York Street
Belfast
BT15 1AQ
Tel: 028 9032 9878
www.etcni.org.uk

Institution of Engineering and Technology (IET)
Michael Faraday House
Stevenage
Hertfordshire
SG1 2AY
Tel: 01438 313 311
www.theiet.org

Tomorrow's Engineers
EngineeringUK

Weston House
246 High Holborn
London
WC1V 7EX
Email: careers@engineeringuk.com
Tel: 020 3206 0400
www.tomorrowsengineers.org.uk

DESIGN ENGINEER

The nature of the work

As a design engineer you could work in a variety of industries, ranging from electronics to synthetic textiles, on projects as diverse as the redesign of a mobile phone to the construction of motorcycle parts from carbon fibre materials.

Your exact duties would depend on the project but could include:

- research – using mathematical modelling to work out whether new developments and innovations would work and be cost effective
- design – turning research ideas into technical plans for prototypes using computer-aided design (CAD) and computer-assisted engineering (CAE) software
- testing – collecting and analysing data from tests on prototypes
- modifying designs and re-testing – this process can go through several stages before a product is ready for manufacture or installation
- reporting – writing or presenting regular progress reports for project managers and clients.

What can you earn?

Starting salaries are between £20,000 and £25,000 a year. Experienced engineers can earn between £26,000 and £40,000. Senior design engineers can earn over £50,000 a year.

Entry requirements

You would normally need a foundation degree, BTEC HNC/HND or degree to become a design engineer.

Mechanical, electrical and civil engineering may also be acceptable to employers.

Contact the Institution of Engineering Designers (IED) and the Institution of Engineering and Technology (IET) for more details of accredited courses, as well as links to engineering careers information.

You may also be able to get into this career starting off as an engineering technician apprentice with a manufacturer or engineering company and then continuing after your Apprenticeship on to higher education qualifications.

To get on to an Apprenticeship, you are likely to need four or five GCSEs (A-C), including maths, English and a science subject.

For more general information about engineering as a career, see the Tomorrow's Engineers website.

More information

SEMTA (Sector Skills Council for Science, Engineering and Manufacturing Technologies in the UK)
14 Upton Road
Watford
Hertfordshire
WD18 0JT
Tel: 0845 643 9001
www.semta.org.uk

Women into Science, Engineering and Construction
Athlone Wing
Old Building
Great Horton Road
Bradford

109

BD7 1AY
Tel: 01274 436485
www.theukrc.org/wise

Tomorrow's Engineers
EngineeringUK
Weston House
246 High Holborn
London
WC1V 7EX
Email: careers@engineeringuk.com
Tel: 020 3206 0400
www.tomorrowsengineers.org.uk

Institution of Engineering Designers
Courtleigh
Westbury Leigh
Westbury
Wiltshire
BA13 3TA
www.ied.org.uk

Engineering Training Council (Northern Ireland)
Interpoint
20-24 York Street
Belfast
BT15 1AQ
Tel: 028 9032 9878
www.etcni.org.uk

Institution of Engineering and Technology
Michael Faraday House
Stevenage
Hertfordshire
SG1 2AY

Tel: 01438 313 311

www.theiet.org

MARINE ENGINEERING TECHNICIAN

The nature of the work

Marine engineering technicians (or shipbuilding technicians) design, build, service and repair boats and ships. They might also perform maintenance on offshore platforms, drilling machinery and equipment.

As a technician, you would use a broad range of engineering skills, such as welding, mechanical and electrical maintenance, and electronic equipment installation. Depending on where you work, your duties could include:

- fault-finding and repairing electronic, hydraulic and mechanical equipment on boats and ships
- assisting in the design and development of new marine equipment
- providing engineering support on board a dive support vessel
- refurbishing older craft with new navigation and communications systems
- using underwater craft (remotely operated vehicles – ROVs) to inspect undersea pipelines
- supervising a team of craftspeople in a ship or boatyard
- maintaining weapons systems, radar and sonar on board Royal Navy warships.
- You would usually work as part of a technical team under the direction of a marine engineer.

What can you earn? Starting salaries can be between £12,000 and £15,000 a year. With experience and qualifications this can rise to between £18,000 and £25,000. Senior technicians can earn over £30,000 a year.

Entry requirements

You could take various routes to becoming a marine technician. You may be able to get into this career as a marine industry apprentice. The range of

Apprenticeships available in your area will depend on the local jobs market and the types of skills employers need from their workers. To get on to an Apprenticeship scheme you may need GCSEs, or equivalent qualifications. To find out more about Apprenticeships, visit the Apprenticeships website.

To get on to an Apprenticeship, you are likely to need four or five GCSEs (A-C), including maths, English and a science subject.

Alternatively, you could take an engineering college course, which would teach you some of the skills needed, such as the BTEC Certificate and Diploma in Mechanical, Electrical or Electronic Engineering. You could also work towards a higher-level qualification, such as a BTEC HNC and HND in Marine Engineering.

You could train as an engineering technician with the Merchant Navy or Royal Navy. After completing your service with them, you could move into the commercial marine engineering industry. Visit the Merchant Navy and Royal Navy websites for more details.

For information about marine engineering as a career, see the Institute of Marine Engineering, Science and Technology (IMarEST) and British Marine Federation websites. For more information about engineering careers, visit the SEMTA website.

More information

SEMTA (Sector Skills Council for Science, Engineering and Manufacturing Technologies in the UK)
14 Upton Road
Watford
Hertfordshire
WD18 0JT
Tel: 0845 643 9001
www.semta.org.uk

Women into Science, Engineering and Construction
UK Resource Centre
Athlone Wing
Old Building
Great Horton Road
Bradford
BD7 1AY
Tel: 01274 436485
www.theukrc.org/wise

Tomorrow's Engineers
EngineeringUK
Weston House
246 High Holborn
London
WC1V 7EX
Email: careers@engineeringuk.com
Tel: 020 3206 0400
www.tomorrowsengineers.org.uk

Institute of Marine Engineering, Science and Technology (IMarEST)
80 Coleman Street
London
EC2R 5BJ
www.imarest.org.uk

Mercahnt Navy Training Board
Carthusian Court
12 Carthusian St
London
EC1M 6EZ
www.mntb.org.uk

British Marine Federation
Marine House

Thorpe Lea Road
Egham
Surrey
TW20 8BF
www.britishmarine.co.uk

Engineering Training Council (Northern Ireland)
Interpoint
20-24 York Street
Belfast
BT15 1AQ
Tel: 028 9032 9878
www.etcni.org.uk

****

9. FARMING AND LAND

Farming is an industry which finds it difficult to find talented recruits at this point in time. The hours are long and the work hard. The industry has gone through significant changes over the years and seeks talented and dedicated people to work within it. the rewards can be significant.

In addition to general farming jobs we look at a range of jobs associated with land management such as countryside rangers and gamekeeprs. the following jobs are outlined:

- Farm Manager
- Farm worker
- Aboriculturalist
- Countryside ranger
- Forest Officer
- Gamekeeper
- Groundperson/Groundskeeper
- Horse Groom
- Horticultural manager

For further information about farming and land jobs go to:

Lantra
Lantra House
Stoneleigh Park
Nr Coventry
Warwickshire
CV8 2LG
Tel: 0845 707 8007
www.lantra.co.uk

FARM MANAGER

The nature of the work

Farm managers run their own businesses or are employed by owners or tenants to run a farm efficiently and profitably. They may run a whole farm or just part of it, such as an arable (crops) unit.

As a farm manager, you could work on one of three main types of farm - livestock (animals), arable (crops) or mixed (animals and crops). Your work would depend partly on the type of farm, but could include:

- planning the running of the farm
- setting budget and production targets
- buying and selling animals or produce
- keeping financial records and records of livestock and/or crops
- recruiting, training and supervising staff.

On smaller farms, you may do practical farm work, such as looking after livestock, driving tractors and other machinery, and harvesting crops. You could also have responsibility for other activities, for example the farm may have a farm shop, horse riding facilities or provide accommodation for tourists. Farm managers work closely with the farm owner and often farm management consultants.

What can you earn?

These figures are only a guide, as actual rates of pay may vary, depending on the employer and where people live.

Minimum wage scales for agricultural work are set each year by the Agricultural Wages Boards for England and Wales. Individual employers may pay more according to the manager's skill and experience.

- Starting salaries for farm managers are at least £20,000 a year
- With experience, farm managers may earn between £26,000 and £30,000.

- The manager of a large farm with over ten years' experience may earn over £50,000 a year.Farm managers may be provided with rent-free accommodation and a vehicle. There may also be other benefits such as farm produce and a pension scheme.

Entry requirements

You will need comprehensive practical farming experience, and will probably start as a supervisor, assistant manager or the manager of a unit, such as dairy or arable.

Most farm managers have a qualification in agriculture. You can do courses at universities and agricultural colleges throughout the UK.

You may be able to get started through an Apprenticeship scheme. The range of Apprenticeships available in your area will depend on the local jobs market and the types of skills employers need from their workers.

Relevant qualifications include:

- City & Guilds Level 4 Diploma in Agricultural Business Management
- Foundation Degree in Agriculture, also available in Agricultural Business Management, Animal Studies, Crop Production.
- BSc (Hons) Degree in Agriculture, also available in areas such as in Agricultural Business Management, Animal Studies, Crop Production.

Entry to a degree course requires at least two A-level grades, normally including chemistry and maths, or another science subject. Alternative equivalent qualifications may be accepted. To search for foundation degrees, HNDs and degrees see the UCAS website. You should check with colleges and universities for entry requirements.

More information

Lantra
Lantra House

Stoneleigh Park
Nr Coventry
Warwickshire
CV8 2LG
Tel: 0845 707 8007
www.lantra.co.uk

City & Guilds
1 Giltspur Street
London
EC1A 9DD
Tel: 0844 543 0000
www.cityandguilds.com

ARBORICULTURALIST

The nature of the work

As an arboriculturalist, your duties will primarily include street or park tree pruning and removals. In some situations, work duties can also include tree planting, hazard tree assessment, diagnosis, and pest control. Work may also include other landscape and non-arboricultural duties.

An arboriculturist's work really begins once they have climbed into the tree. In addition to tree pruning, branch removal and felling, arboriculturists may also undertake work such as cable bracing to maintain the health of trees and inspections to assess the health of trees. Work is usually done from a rope and harness but may involve the use of elevated work platforms ('cherry-pickers').

An arboriculturist's duties may also include landscape and other non-arboricultural responsibilities such as tree and shrub planting and maintenance and snow removal.

What can you earn?

Arboriculturalists can earn between £18,000 and over £25,000 a year.

Entry requirements

If you are interested in becoming an arboricultural climber it is important that you:
- enjoy working outside
- have a good head for heights
- enjoy practical/physical work.

Individuals becoming climbers are likely have worked in the industry, usually as a groundworker or general arboricultural worker. Some may enter the industry having undertaken a full-time training programme and so already have some experience of climbing.

More information

Lantra
Lantra House
Stoneleigh Park
Nr Coventry
Warwickshire
CV8 2LG
Tel: 0845 707 8007
www.lantra.co.uk

Royal Forestry Society (RFS)
www.rfs.org.uk

International Society of Arboriculture (ISA)
www.isa-arbor.com

Institute of Chartered Foresters (ICF)
59 George Street
Edinburgh
EH2 2JG
Tel: 0131 240 1425
www.charteredforesters.org

The Arboricultural Association
Ullenwood Court
Ullenwood
Cheltenham
Gloucestershire
GL53 9QS
Tel 01242 522152
www.trees.org.uk

FARM WORKER

The nature of the work

Your work will vary depending on the type of farm and the time of year, but can include:

- looking after animals - such as feeding, cleaning (mucking out), caring for sick animals and using a milking machine to milk cows
- ploughing fields, sowing, looking after and harvesting crops, spreading fertiliser and spraying crops
- driving and looking after tractors, combine harvesters and other vehicles
- maintenance of farm buildings
- laying and trimming hedges
- digging and maintaining ditches
- putting up and mending fences.

You would be supervised by the farm owner, manager, supervisor or landowner, and you may also supervise casual staff. You will often need technical agricultural knowledge to understand the tasks you carry out.Most jobs involve working outdoors in all weather conditions. Farm work can be dirty and dusty and may not suit people who suffer from allergies such as hay fever.

What can you earn?

Rates of pay may vary, depending on the employer and where people live, however there is a minimum wage for those working in England and Wales (set by the Agricultural Wages Board).

Farm workers usually earn at least £7239 a year at age 16, and £9795 a year at age 19. Those over 19 years of age usually earn at least £14,986 a year, and experienced farm workers may earn up to £19,000 a year. Individual employers may pay more depending on skills and experience. Many farm workers can be given free or low rent accommodation, or a lodging allowance. Overtime may also be available.

Entry requirements

You do not need any particular qualifications for starting in this job, but it helps to have an interest in farming. It would also help you if you have experience of working on a farm, either through work experience or a weekend or holiday job.

You may be able to start this work through an Apprenticeship scheme. You will need to check which schemes are available in your area. To find out more, see the Apprenticeships website.

You could also take short courses, such as on how to operate a particular piece of agricultural equipment, tractor driving or fork lift operation.

If your job involves tasks such as operating chainsaws and using pesticides, you will need to have relevant certificates of competence as a legal requirement. These are awarded by City & Guilds Land-based Services and by Lantra Awards. See their websites for more information.

More information

Lantra Awards
www.lantra-awards.co.uk

Lantra
Lantra House
Stoneleigh Park
Nr Coventry
Warwickshire
CV8 2LG
Tel: 0845 707 8007
www.lantra.co.uk

City & Guilds
1 Giltspur Street
London
EC1A 9DD
Tel: 0844 543 0000
www.cityandguilds.com

Department for Environment, Food & Rural Affairs (DEFRA)
www.defra.gov.uk

COUNTRYSIDE RANGER

The nature of the work
As a countryside ranger, your work could include:

- planning and creating habitats to conserve plants and animals
- tree planting, pond management and other practical tasks
- making sure that footpaths, bridleways and waterways meet health and safety recommendations
- carrying out field surveys to detect changes in the environment
- patrolling sites to help visitors and to discourage poaching or damage to the environment
- giving talks
- managing exhibitions and resource centres
- leading guided walks
- taking part in community projects
- working with local landowners and businesses whose activities may affect the environment
- keeping records and writing reports.

You could specialise in a particular area such as habitat management, fieldwork or education, or in certain types of habitat such as waterways, coasts or moorlands.

What can you earn?

In local authorities, rangers can earn from around £18,000 to over £25,000 a year. Senior Rangers can earn over £30,000 a year. Salaries with other employers vary considerably.

Entry requirements

Before starting work as a countryside ranger you will usually need a relevant qualification and work experience. A good way to get experience is by volunteering with organisations such as:

- a Wildlife Trust
- the National Trust
- BTCV
- the Forestry Commission
- Groundwork UK.

See organisations' websites for details. Some run training courses for their volunteers.

The qualifications you need before starting a paid job will vary depending on the employer and the amount of experience you have. Relevant qualifications include:

- BTEC Level 3 Certificate/Diploma in Countryside Management
- BTEC HNC/HND in Environmental Conservation
- Diploma in Work-Based Environmental Conservation
- Environmental Conservation Apprenticeship
- foundation degrees in subjects such as countryside management and conservation
- degrees in subjects such as countryside management, rural environmental management, conservation and environment, or environmental studies.

For all courses you should check entry requirements with individual colleges or universities.

To search for foundation degree, HND and degree courses, see the UCAS (Universities and Colleges Admissions Service) website.

You may be able to start this job through an Apprenticeship scheme. You will need to check which schemes are available in your area. To find out more, see the Apprenticeships website.

More information
LGcareers (local government careers)
www.lgcareers.com

Lantra
Lantra House
Stoneleigh Park
Nr Coventry
Warwickshire
CV8 2LG
Tel: 0845 707 8007
www.lantra.co.uk

Wildlife Trusts
www.wildlifetrusts.org

National Trust
www.nationaltrust.org.uk

Groundwork UK
www.groundwork.org.uk

BTCV
Sedum House
Mallard Way
Potteric Carr
Doncaster
DNL 8DB
Tel: 01302 388883
www.btcv.org.uk

Forestry Commission
www.forestry.gov.uk

Countryside Management Association (CMA)
Writtle College
Lordship Road
Writtle
Chelmsford
Essex
CM1 3RR
Tel: 01245 424116
www.countrysidemanagement.org.uk

FOREST OFFICER

The nature of the work

A forest officer may have progressed from a working role in the woodland into this more managerial position. Where several woodlands are owned, or managed, a forest officer may be responsible for each individual woodland, with a head forester overseeing the work in all of the woodlands.

Working in private woodland or for the Forestry Commission will often require a wider range of skills and knowledge including land management skills. The forest officer will also usually have to control a budget and follow a business plan developed for the sites they manage. They will be answerable in the first instance to the head forester, who will oversee the forestry work on a number of different locations.

Their main tasks may include planning the work to be carried out by staff and contractors, managing the maintenance of machinery and equipment, maintaining records of work and ensuring that heath and safety policies are observed.

They will also be required to survey and inspect trees and sites, selecting and marking up timber to be harvested as well as planning, monitoring and evaluating habitat management work.

Forest officers are also known as foresters, forest managers, woodland managers and assistant head foresters.

What can you earn?

Salaries can range from around £19,000 to around £30,000 a year.

Entry requirements

Individuals entering at this level will have significant experience in forestry and will usually have completed a higher level qualification in forestry or related subjects. They may also have completed the relevant certificates of competence for their work area. These might include chainsaw use, chipper use and operation of specialist equipment such as a forwarder or harvester.

More information

Lantra
Lantra House
Stoneleigh Park
Nr Coventry
Warwickshire
CV8 2LG
Tel: 0845 707 8007
www.lantra.co.uk

Royal Forestry Society (RFS)
www.rfs.org.uk

Forestry Commission
www.forestry.gov.uk

Institute of Chartered Foresters
59 George Street
Edinburgh
EH2 2JG
Tel: 0131 240 1425
www.charteredforesters.org

BTCV
Sedum House
Mallard Way
Potteric Carr
Doncaster
DNL 8DB
Tel: 01302 388883
www.btcv.org.uk

The Arboricultural Association
Ullenwood Court
Ullenwood
Cheltenham
Gloucestershire
GL53 9QS
Tel 01242 522152
www.trees.org.uk

GAMEKEEPER

The nature of the work
Your work would vary according to the season, but your main tasks would include:

- organising shoots and fishing parties
- hiring and supervising staff such as beaters (who flush out birds during shoots)
- keeping records of what is shot or caught and arranging the sale of game
- training gun dogs and working with them
- breeding game birds for release in the wild
- controlling predators such as foxes, crows and rats by shooting and trapping
- protecting game from poachers by patrolling the beat area at night
- repairing equipment, buildings and game pens and cleaning guns

127

- clearing woodland and burning heather
- liaising with the police to deal with crime such as badger digging and hare coursing.

As a keeper protecting and managing rivers and streams as habitats for trout and salmon you would be known as a river keeper or ghillie.

What can you earn?

Gamekeepers can earn from £11,000 to around £18,000 a year.
Employers often provide free or cheap accommodation and a vehicle.
Figures are intended as a guideline only.

Entry requirements
You would usually start your career as a gamekeeper by working as an assistant or under-keeper, working with an experienced keeper.

Competition for vacancies is strong, so it will be useful if you have some paid or unpaid experience, perhaps as part of a beating team, or in a related area such as forestry or farming. Practical skills such as carpentry would also be useful. You would need a driving licence for most jobs.

You could prepare for work as a gamekeeper by doing a relevant full-time course before looking for work, although this is not essential. Courses include:
- BTEC (Edexcel) Level 3 Certificate or Diploma in Countryside Management.
- SQA National Certificate Introduction to Gamekeeping (in Scotland)
- SQA Higher National Certificate in Gamekeeping and Wildlife Management (in Scotland).

You should check with individual colleges for their entry requirements. See the 'Links' section of the National Gamekeepers Organisation Educational Trust website for a list of some of the colleges running gamekeeping courses.
You may be able to get into this job through an Apprenticeship scheme. The range of Apprenticeships available in your area will depend on the local jobs market and the types of skills employers need from their workers. For more information, visit the Apprenticeships website.

More information

National Gamekeepers Organisation
www.nationalgamekeepers.org.uk

Scottish Gamekeepers Association
www.scottishgamekeepers.co.uk

GROUNDS PERSON OR GREEN KEEPER

The nature of the work
Your main responsibility would be to manage the soil and grass to make sure the turf is always in top condition. Your duties would typically include:

- preparing land for turf laying
- applying nutrients
- rolling and mowing the turf
- identifying and controlling weeds
- setting out and marking lines on surfaces
- installing and maintaining equipment like nets, posts and protective covers
- ensuring irrigation and drainage systems are maintained
- looking after surrounding areas - decorative displays, concrete or tarmac
- operating equipment like hedge cutters, strimmers and ride-on mowers
- painting, removing rubbish and carrying out general duties
- maintaining good communication with your customers

Your tasks would vary according to the season and weather conditions.

What can you earn?

Salary scales for this work can be:
Groundsperson: £14,985 to £18,310 a year
Skilled groundsperson: £18,700 to £22,850
Head groundsperson: £24,445 to £31,795.

There may be bonuses and payment for overtime, and accommodation is sometimes provided.

Entry requirements

If you have experience in horticulture, you could find work as an unskilled groundsperson without relevant qualifications. You may then be able to progress to skilled level by gaining experience and working towards qualifications.

Alternatively, you could start by doing a course that would help you develop the skills needed for the job. Relevant courses include:

- Certificate/Diploma in Horticulture at levels 2 and 3
- Certificate/Diploma in Sports and Amenity Turf Maintenance at Level 2.
- Entry requirements for courses vary, so you should check directly with colleges.
- A driving licence will be useful for some jobs.
- You may be able to get into this job through an Apprenticeship scheme. The range of Apprenticeships available in your area will depend on the local jobs market and the types of skills employers need from their workers.

More information

Lantra
Lantra House
Stoneleigh Park
Nr Coventry
Warwickshire
CV8 2LG
Tel: 0845 707 8007
www.lantra.co.uk

Institute of Groundsmanship (IOG)
28 Stratford Office Village
Wolverton Mill East
Milton Keynes

MK12 5TW
Tel: 01908 312511
www.iog.org

British and International Golf Greenkeepers Association Limited (BIGGA)
BIGGA HOUSE
Aldwark
Alne
York
YO61 1UF
Tel:+44(0)1347 833800
Fax:+44(0)1347 833801
Email:info@bigga.co.uk
www.bigga.org.uk

HORSE GROOM

The nature of the work
As a groom, you would:
- provide food and water for horses
- replace bedding
- clean equipment such as saddles and bridles ('tack')
- clean, brush and sometimes clip, horses' coats
- muck out stables
- check for changes in the condition of horses and report problems
- treat minor wounds, change dressings and give medication
- follow instructions from vets when treatment is needed.

You may also be responsible for exercising the horses each day.
If you work with show jumpers or race horses, you will prepare them for events, and may accompany them. In studs and breeding yards you will work with stallions, mares and foals, and may help vets to deliver foals. In riding schools you may greet clients, lead riders out on foot, and accompany them on horseback.

What can you earn?

Grooms can start at around £12,500 a year
Experienced grooms can earn around £16,000
Head lads/girls in a racing yard can earn £20,000 or more.
Some employers provide accommodation, food, free stabling for your own horse and riding lessons.

Entry requirements

You must be at least 16, and there may be weight restrictions for some jobs. Although you may not need qualifications, employers may prefer you to have experience, and some may ask for a nationally-recognised qualification such as:

- BTEC Level 2 Certificate and Diploma in Horse Care
- BTEC Level 3 Diploma in Horse Management
- British Horse Society (BHS) Stage 1 in Horse Knowledge and Care
- Association of British Riding Schools (ABRS) Preliminary Horse Care and Riding Certificate.

For BHS or ABRS qualifications you must be at least 16, and would usually need experience of handling and riding horses. Visit the BHS and ABRS websites for details.

You could get practical experience as a volunteer, for example helping out at a local stable. This could give you an advantage when looking for paid work.

You can train in race-horse care at the British Racing School in Newmarket and the Northern Racing College in Doncaster. You will not need riding experience to start, as there is a non-rider option up to NVQ level 2. However, most trainees do ride.
If you are interested in the horse breeding industry, you can train at the National Stud in Newmarket or at other training centres. See the Thoroughbred Breeders' Association website for details.

You may be able to get into this job through an Apprenticeship scheme. The range of Apprenticeships available in your area will depend on the local jobs